"In this lyrical and brilliant memoir, Benjamin Taylor investigates his childhood with piercing clarity and unapologetic nostalgia. His insights are wise, his sense of humor always in evidence, and his yearning for lost time exquisitely palpable. Reading this book is like reading all of Proust in just under two hundred pages. It is an utterly enchanting little masterpiece."   —Andrew Solomon

"A witty, painful, uninhibited memoir of, ostensibly, one year of childhood. Within his chosen focus, Taylor achieves a necessary feat of autobiography: The child who grew and the adult who more than remembers live together as one on the page. You encounter vitalistic youth; and sense there, also, the wing of mortality. Taylor's *Hue and Cry* is a vast offer of thanks and glowing triumph, his masterpiece to date."   —Richard Howard

"Benjamin Taylor enchanted readers by his *Tales Out of School*. He has done it again. *The Hue and Cry at Our House*, a short elegiac memoir that moves gracefully between the fateful year of President Kennedy's assassination, when Taylor was eleven, and other moments of searing significance in Taylor's life, is wondrously candid and deeply moving."   —Louis Begley

"In his keen focus on the 1963 death of John F. Kennedy in Dallas, Benjamin Taylor returns to the morning of the assassination in his hometown of Fort Worth when he had the dazzling experience, as a schoolboy, of shaking the hand of the President, his hero. This acute, intense memoir achieves the stature of national as well as personal elegy, a breathtaking accomplishment, classical and impassioned. It belongs to the best American literature of idealism and loss, a profoundly eloquent reading of our mid-century history and its heartbroken legacy to this day." —Patricia Hampl

"Benjamin Taylor's memoir is an American classic but also a Proustian classic: exquisitely attuned to the nuances of adolescence, and to the experience of being an outsider in a world of conventional manners and expectations. It is rare, outside of Proust's fiction, to find such fearless candor in a consummate prose stylist." —Judith Thurman

"What was it like to be a gifted, gay, upper-middle-class Jewish kid (with a touch of Asperger Syndrome) in 1964 Fort Worth, Texas? The answer is brilliantly explicated in Ben Taylor's memoir, *The Hue and Cry at Our House*, which begins with the assassination of JFK (Taylor shook the President's hand a few hours before Dealey Plaza) and gains momentum from there. That the author will grow up to be one of our most elegant, multifaceted writers is the final turn of the screw."
—Blake Bailey, author of *Cheever: A Life* and *The Splendid Things We Planned*

"Reaching the last page of *The Hue and Cry at Our House*, I found myself marveling that such a slender volume could contain so much wisdom and emotion. Benjamin Taylor writes in beautiful, precise prose about his younger self and his older self, about his parents and his friends, about a life lived over time, and about all our lives lived over time. This is a mesmerizing memoir."

—Margot Livesey

"Memory. History. Loss. Love. These are the themes of Ben Taylor's haunting *Hue and Cry at Our House*. A beautiful book about finding meaning by sifting through the past."

—David Ebershoff,
author of *The Danish Girl* and *The 19th Wife*

"Taylor has painted a gem-like portrait, in delicate colors and with fine detail, of a childhood in genteel Fort Worth at the end of the Kennedy era, and has written an honest and moving account of a mercurial boy's struggle to be himself."

—Caleb Crain

PRAISE FOR
Proust: The Search

"A marvel of brief biography."

—Thomas Mallon, *The New York Times Book Review*

"Those who found reading Proust too grand an undertaking over the years because of distractions and deficiencies of their own, might well rush to reconsider after confronting this dazzlingly elegant biography."

—Philip Roth

"Taylor's slim and elegant biography will bring new readers to Proust, and remind us to see him as truly modern."

—Ingrid Wassenaar, *The Times Literary Supplement*

"Because Taylor has been willing to learn from Proust how to write his biography—be enjoyably clever but not too presumptuous—his book is unusually instructive about how we can read Proust.... Explains both formally and intimately, through straightforward documentary narrative and engaging interpretation, the facts and fictions of Proust's extraordinarily improbable life."

—Adam Phillips, *London Review of Books*

"Deeply researched, and immensely well considered, Benjamin Taylor's own search is an outstanding addition to Proust studies."

—Robert McCrum, *The Observer* (London)

PRAISE FOR
Naples Declared: A Walk Around the Bay

"Splendid."   —Stacy Schiff, author of *Cleopatra: A Life*

"There is no more witty, worldly, cultivated, or amiably candid observer imaginable than Benjamin Taylor. This book belongs on the shelf of the very best literary travel guides."

—Phillip Lopate,
author of *Waterfront: A Walk Around Manhattan*

"Erudite and charming, *Naples Declared* is a remarkable book; it's about place and history and survival; it's fresh, it's wise, and it's not to be missed."

—Brenda Wineapple, author of *White Heat: The Friendship of Emily Dickinson and Thomas Wentworth Higginson*

PENGUIN BOOKS

THE HUE AND CRY
AT OUR HOUSE

THE HUE AND CRY
AT OUR HOUSE

A Year Remembered

BENJAMIN TAYLOR

PENGUIN BOOKS

PENGUIN BOOKS

An imprint of Penguin Random House LLC
375 Hudson Street
New York, New York 10014
penguin.com

PHOTOGRAPH CREDITS:
Page facing page 1: The University of Texas at Arlington Library Special Collections, Page 175: Courtesy, Beth-El Congregation Archives, Fort Worth, Other photographs courtesy of the author

LIBRARY OF CONGRESS CATALOGING-IN-PUBLICATION DATA
Names: Taylor, Benjamin, 1952– author.
Title: The hue and cry at our house : a year remembered /
Benjamin Taylor.
Description: New York : Penguin books, [2017] |
Description based on print version record and CIP data provided by publisher;
resource not viewed.
Identifiers: LCCN 2016054540 (print) | LCCN 2016049441 (ebook) |
ISBN 9781524705299 (ebook) | ISBN 9780143131649 (paperback)
Subjects: LCSH: Taylor, Benjamin, 1952– | Authors, American—
20th century—Biography.
Classification: LCC PS3570.A92714 (print) |
LCC PS3570.A92714 Z46 2017 (ebook) | DDC 813/.54 [B]—dc23
LC record available at https://lccn.loc.gov/2016054540

Printed in the United States of America
1   3   5   7   9   10   8   6   4   2

Set in Janson

For you, P.

We all live in suspense, from day to day, from hour to hour; in other words, we are the hero of our own story.

—MARY McCARTHY

Contents

Preface

One year suffices. I've tried to wrest from the stream of time what happened to the Taylors and the nation between November 1963 and November 1964. But any twelve months could stand for the whole. Our years are so implicated in one another that the least important is important enough. In act three of Thornton Wilder's Our Town, *Emily Webb Gibbs has died and been brought to the Grover's Corners burial ground, joining the taciturn, unempathic, all-knowing dead who sit together in rows. New to eternity and homesick for life,*

The four of us, autumn, 1952.

she asks her mother-in-law, Mrs. Gibbs, whether she can go back and relive one day. "Choose an unimportant day," says Mother Gibbs, who thinks the whole idea unwise. "It will be important enough." Emily chooses February 11, 1899, a bitter-cold Tuesday: her twelfth birthday.

"Do you want any special time of day?" asks the Stage Manager. "Oh, I want the whole day!" Emily says.

Standing invisibly in the family kitchen, watching her parents at their morning routines, she cannot look hard enough, since in a single day are all the days. How unbearably beautiful Mama and Papa are. And how oblivious, whereas their omniscient daughter sees the whole future—in which they'll lose their son, Wally, whose appendix is going to burst on a camping trip to Crawford Notch, and lose Emily when she dies giving birth to a second child. Life is poised to strip the Webbs clean. "Just for a moment we're all together," Emily says, "just for a moment let's be happy," though of course her parents, busy with breakfast, don't hear.

"Take me back—up the hill—to my grave," she says sadly to the Stage Manager, then asks him if the living ever comprehend life while they're living it.

"*No—Saints and poets, maybe—they do some.*"

An unsanctified, unpoetical life like mine is lived in the blind alleys, makeshifts, work-arounds, long cuts, fool's errands—all the unforeseeables of a decent run. But you get one temperament only and it ramifies through all the decades. Any year I chose would show the same mettle, the same frailties stamping me at eleven and twelve.

The Hue and Cry
at Our House

In front of the Hotel Texas, Fort Worth,
November 22, 1963, 8:30 A.M.

CHAPTER ONE

No Faint Hearts

He shook my hand! This hand!" I announced, holding it aloft as I reeled into class. With the tiniest of smiles Mrs. Westbrook directed me to my seat. The Phoenicians were under discussion. She'd written "Byblos" and "Tyre" on the chalkboard. "Prior to the high civilization of the Greeks, boys and girls, prior to the triumphs of Rome, there flourished a maritime people situated *here*," and she yanked down the map and took up her pointer to indicate the eastern Mediterranean.

"Phoenicia gave us"—she paused pedagogically—"the alphabet. But history isn't only what happened long ago. It can be shaking a President's hand this morning." And saying so she smiled with all her teeth, at me.

On this Friday as on every other, our principal, Mr. Singleton, came onto the public-address system to say, "Teachers, the ghost is walking," a deep mystery until Mrs. Westbrook explained that it was code for "Your paychecks have arrived." But this was Friday, November 22, 1963, and it was history that was walking. In preparation for the big day of President Kennedy's visit to Fort Worth, we'd memorized the names of all thirty-four of his predecessors, pictures of whom ran around the space above the chalkboard. Those pesky ones between Jackson and Lincoln gave me trouble, as did those between Lincoln and TR.

Lincoln was Mrs. Westbrook's passion. She'd rounded off our presidential unit with a reading of "O Captain! My Captain!" About most of these flabby-faced monuments we were left to draw our own conclusions. Warren Harding resembled Dr.

Schwarz, my pediatrician. William McKinley was the guy behind the counter of the hardware store. In his vest with white piping, Woodrow Wilson had an undertaker look. William Howard Taft, the only smiler, appeared as rotund and crinkly-eyed and fake-jovial as poor Uncle Isadore, destined for a bad end. (About Isadore Wolchansky, unaffectionately called "Walnuts" at our house, more later.) I spotted James Buchanan as one who cracks a silly joke while slipping a hand down your pants.

Thelma Westbrook wielded her opinions unanswerably. If she said "O Captain! My Captain!" was the greatest poem, that was that. Around her were arcana I hadn't the temerity to look into: What did Mr. Westbrook do? Did they have children? What street did they live on? It would have seemed a profanation to wonder about her life apart from us. Did she sleep in her socks? We could as soon picture the goddess Minerva cooking breakfast as Mrs. Westbrook.

Life had never been better than on that Friday morning. Fort Worth was the center of the universe and I was in the best sixth-grade class of

Westcliff Elementary, where the Westbrook ruled and I was her darling. "One of your mothers tells me that her child *sheds tears* over his homework!" she'd announced earlier that autumn, a reproach to the sluggards among us. Treasonable of Mom to have revealed that and I told her so. Tears over what? I try now to recall. Surely not Phoenicia or Walt Whitman. Math, no doubt, and the child was father to the man: I count on my fingers to this day.

A repellently good boy like most of my kind, Jewish and going-to-be-homosexual, I seemed all the more so by comparison with Floyd Hickey, for instance, who liked opening his fly to show girls the goods—for which outrage he'd been not just spanked but beaten by the ordinarily lenient Mr. Singleton. It hadn't worked. Back in class next day Floyd sat there smiling in bitter triumph. A tough kid, surely now in prison or dead. And I was his opposite, high-minded and with the testimony of tears over homework to prove it.

It was unusual for me to be late to class, even when coping with asthma, as I usually was. (Thirty minutes on the nebulizer before school were routine.)

But that morning had been a once-in-a-lifetime opportunity, countenanced beforehand by Mrs. Westbrook: I'd been to the rally in front of the Hotel Texas. Mom woke me before dawn and we dressed and ate a hasty breakfast. We were determined to go despite heavy rain. The event exists on audiotape and in still shots. I remember an elderly lady beside me with a homemade placard: KENNEDY 1964! GOLDWATER 1864! This made me crumple up with laughter. Less friendly homemade placards would greet the President later that morning. At the Dallas airport one of them read VOTE RIGHT! VOTE WHITE! ANYONE BUT THE NAACP'S KENNEDY!

Many of the ladies out front of the Hotel Texas have on rain bonnets, but the umbrellas are mostly down. The foul weather of earlier that morning has let up. *"There are no faint hearts in Fort Worth!"* John F. Kennedy declares to us from a platform mounted on a truck. He sounds like nobody we've heard before: the domed vowels, the rapid stately cadences, the victorious hammering home of point after point. He isn't Ike. As the drizzle tapers he says: "What we're trying to do in this country and what we're trying to do around the world is, I believe, quite simple, and that is to build a military structure which will defend the vital interests of the United States. And in that great cause, as it did in World War Two, as it did in developing the best bomber system in the world, the B-58, and as it will now do in developing the best fighter system in the world, the TFX, *Fort Worth will play its proper part!*" Mad cheering from us. He comes down from the platform to shake our outstretched hands. A file photo from that moment captures Mom looking very happy under her rain bonnet. Indeed, almost every face in the interracial throng is happy. It seems that the President is looking right at my mother. (Taking a fancy to her? I like to think so.) Directly in front of Mom, there I am—obscured by the head of a Secret Service agent but recognizable by my meticulously parted hair.

That five-minute speech was a sketch of the somewhat longer address the President would immediately give to an elite breakfast crowd in the hotel ballroom. (It was the room in which my parents had been married twenty-three years earlier.) Mom wanted Dad to spring for tickets to the indoor event. But he'd always been suspicious of the Kennedys' mystique and huge millions. "I didn't have a rich daddy like Jack Kennedy. Everything I've got, I *earned*!"

Mom and I were the Kennedy lovers in the house.

She kept a copy of *Profiles in Courage* on her desk. (It crossed few minds at the time that this Pulitzer Prize winner might have been ghostwritten for Kennedy.) From Mrs. Kennedy's televised White House tour Mom had learned simply to put flowers in a vase rather than arrange them. Taped to the door of my bedroom was the Inaugural Address exhorting us to ask what we could do for our country.

On the platform this Apollo with his copper-colored hair, blue eyes and tanned complexion made a comic contrast to the raincoated, pasty, glamour-free men who surrounded him as he spoke, one of whom would be sworn in as the new President several hours later.

I recall that sometime between two and three

that afternoon, we on the playground saw Mr. Singleton take down the flag, then raise it again to half-staff. When we got back to class Mrs. Westbrook was seated at her desk. She had taken off her glasses and appeared to us half naked. She rose. "Boys and girls . . ." A sob came out. She put her hand to her mouth and turned to the board. A couple of the nicest girls—Mimi (Emily) Anderson and Carrie Harrington—began to cry too, without needing to know why. Now Mrs. Westbrook turned to face us. She hooked her glasses first behind one ear, then behind the other. "Boys and girls, a very great man died in Dallas today."

Dallas was a long way off, more than thirty miles. I'd been there only a few times. It was either east or west of Fort Worth. I could never remember. The only great man I could think of over there was the popular mayor, Earle Cabell, scion of a dairy and convenience-store fortune. Must be that Earle Cabell had died.

Then she told us. But I had shaken John F. Kennedy's hand that morning and seen for myself that he was indestructible. And the words from Mrs. Westbrook's mouth made no sense.

Westcliff Elementary. There all of us had lined up in the spring of 1961 to receive, in fluted pastry cups, Sabin's polio-vanquishing sugar cube. A number of my early memories have to do with polio. In what must be my very earliest, I am struggling to escape Dr. Schwarz, who comes at me with an enormous hypodermic of Salk's inactivated virus. Looks like buttermilk in the barrel, feels like lead when he drives it in. I shriek for all I'm worth.

Nearly as primordial is this, dating from when I was three or four: We're boarding the Texas Zephyr for Denver. Daddy waves us—my mother, grandmother, brother and me—out of the station. It is a year or two before vaccinations; the traditional summer fear exercises all its dread power; everyone knows at least one family that's been devastated by infantile paralysis. We're on our way to the supposed safety of Colorado's higher altitude. In our sleeping compartment Mom attaches a ready-made tie to me while my brother, ten years older, knots his own. She and Bubbe (Little Bubbe, my mother's mother; my father's mother is Big Bubbe) put on hats and gloves, and verify the contents of their handbags, and we make our way, swayed and jolted, to the dining car with its starched pink tablecloths, where little glass vials attached between the windows hold trembling carnations.

Here memory winks out, though I pick it up again when we're back in our compartment and I'm curled against Little Bubbe's ample flank in the upper berth, crying. There's a night-light up there and a nylon mesh in which to secure belongings. Earlier, when the porter had opened the berth with his intriguing key, he assured the little boy there was nothing to fear. But I'm convinced this strange drawer will close up on Bubbe and me.

The scene changes. We are at Pike's Peak. I'm feasting on saltwater taffy while Tommy (who liked courting a little danger) eyes the mountain and tells our grandmother he's going to climb it.

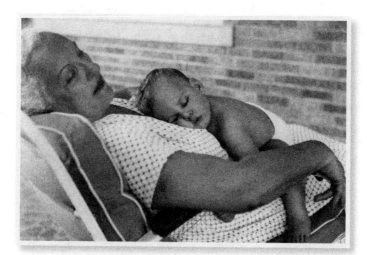

Napping with Little Bubbe.

A slightly later memory pertains to one of the few times I got spanked: My parents are dressing to go to a party. I'm four. The summer heat is overwhelming. I'm outdoors, drinking from the garden hose. Daddy's new car, a 1956 cream-and-red Buick Special, is in the driveway. In obedience to a brainstorm, I roll up three of the windows all the way and the fourth almost, stick the hose through and blithely come indoors. My parents kiss me in the kitchen, leave the housekeeper a number where they'll be, go to the car. They're instantly back. Daddy's rage is uncontainable. Mommy just keeps asking why, why I've done such a naughty thing. They imagine it's because I don't want them to go to their party.

In fact they do go, in the other car, but not before I get it good. How can they, grown-ups, understand that the motive was nothing so calculated as wanting them to remain at home? I remember my thinking clearly: The day has been hot. The leather upholstery of the new car needs cooling down. I am doing them a favor.

That autumn Daddy's ruined Buick Special was replaced by an Oldsmobile 98 sedan. I entered Mrs. Pakston's kindergarten at Westcliff, straightened up, flew right. But I'd left Mom and Dad with a little taste of chaos and old night. Between us, thenceforth, the assurances would be only provisional.

I wonder whether I've learned as much since leaving Westcliff as I did under the tutelage of Mmes. Pakston, Bassinger, Pinson, Pyburn, Kirk and, above all, Westbrook. These dedicated educators, for without exception they were, opened my eyes on an ever larger world. I learned who Johannes Kepler was and who was Michael Faraday. And the difference between stalactites and stalagmites. Mrs. Canafax, in charge of music, introduced us to Haydn's Surprise Symphony and Copland's *Appalachian Spring*. Under the guidance of Mrs. Everett, our art teacher, we discovered pictures—Fra Filippo Lippi's *Annunciation*, Vermeer's *Girl with the Red Hat*, Millet's *The Gleaners*, van Gogh's *Sunflowers*, Thomas Moran's *Grand Canyon of the Colorado River*. For theatrics we put on *Spoon River Anthology*. Mrs. Westbrook assigned me the following words to speak: "I am Anne Rutledge who sleep beneath these weeds, beloved in life of Abraham Lincoln, wedded to him, not through union, but through separation. Bloom forever, O Republic, from the dust of my bosom!" I wondered how I was going to get through it. Several girls were just as nervous about the men's epitaphs they were assigned. But the show went beautifully.

I walked home from school that fatal November Friday to find everybody crying. In the kitchen, Otta Mae Lowe, our housekeeper, did so calmly as she organized dinner. Brushing past me, Dad walked out on his own tears as I came into the living room. Mom took me in her arms. Fresh from her regular Friday shampoo and set, she wore the particular fragrance of Mam'zelle's, her beauty parlor.

"If it had gone on raining—" I ventured, but she put a finger to my lips. If it had gone on raining the assassin would have been firing on a closed and armored car.

We were a family expert in the ifs. Two years earlier in my father's hometown, Tyler, a hundred forty miles east of Fort Worth, on the first cold night of autumn, a faulty furnace had set the family house ablaze, killing three of my cousins, Barbara, Lisa and Tanya, and Big Bubbe. Aunt Beatrice, called Pesh, my father's beloved older sister and mother of the three girls, survived but was so damaged from smoke inhalation that she never spoke another coherent word. And she seemed not to remember her children, the only mercy in this tale. My uncle Max got through the fire unscathed, which enraged my father. He developed a suspicion, with what basis in fact none of us knew, that Max, always so handy around the house, had fixed the furnace himself and thereby caused the fire. Over the years I have come to think Dad was right, but on no more evidence than he possessed. Uncle Max died eight years later of bowel cancer, having faithfully cared for Aunt Pesh, who lived another eleven years.

When something this terrible happens to a family, it is either spoken about continually or not at all. We were of the not-at-all school, but now I see that the four dead of that night, along with Aunt

Pesh, sat down nightly with us. There were no faint hearts at 4149 Ranier Court. But all roads led to and from the fire. The hue and cry at our house was against disorder, bedevilment, despair. My parents meant to outrun those beasts. If we'd had an escutcheon, VIGOR (our young President's favorite word) would have been the motto it bore. But blow by blow, life builds you a tragic outlook.

Friday was, as I say, my mother's standing appointment at Mam'zelle's. Maxine was her "beauty operator," as they were called. I would sometimes, when younger, be taken along to that paradise of femininity: the addictive aromas of Aqua Net and nail polish, the babbling brook of ladies' small talk, so much more interesting than the large talk of men. Among the leading hairdressers at Mam'zelle's were Wayman and DeWayne. These oddly named men were of a kind unfamiliar to me. I recall that Daddy would not allow either to touch a hair of Mom's head. Anyhow, nothing could stand in the way of this Friday routine. Maxine had told Mom the news from Dallas when she came through the door for her one-o'clock. Wash, set and manicure took place while the radio gave updates on the President from Parkland Hospital.

From that Friday I have dreaded weekends. A disproportionate evil is crowded into them. A little after nightfall at Andrews Air Force Base the new leader asks, in a glare of klieg lights, for our help and God's. On Saturday the dead President is taken to the Capitol where he lies in state. On Sunday the assassin is assassinated on live TV. "Just grateful the killer wasn't a Jew," Daddy said as soon as Oswald was named. But the killer's killer, Jack Ruby, *is* Jewish and the local press are promptly calling him "Rubenstein." On Monday the caisson, followed by a riderless stallion, makes its way from the White House to Saint Matthew's Cathedral. There's Charles de Gaulle in plain khaki, towering over the crowd. And beside him Haile Selassie, unsuitably covered in medals and ribands. Now the dry-eyed Kennedys, majestic as Romans in a frieze, make their way down the Cathedral steps. A planet stops when the little son salutes.

CHAPTER TWO

A CLEAN BURROW

In the early months of 1963 I'd fallen seriously ill. My asthma led to a bronchitis that turned into pneumonia. We had Dr. Cohen, old Dr. Schwarz's successor, coming daily to the house, and a nurse was hired. I wasn't scared, just tired of battling for the next breath. Every part of my body hurt from the days and nights of fever. I remember asking my mother if she thought I might die. She told me I was silly and left the room in a hurry, with her hand on her mouth. My brother came in and gave me a long, tight hug. This, too, was a bad sign.

Then my fever broke, my breathing eased, and I went back to school. That was fifth grade. The scholarly promised land of Mrs. Westbrook's classroom was not yet mine. I was stuck with Mr. Dreasley, who belonged to the John Birch Society. He talked to us about the need for every family to have its own bomb shelter. Weathering thermonuclear war wouldn't be as hard as people imagined. A clean burrow stocked with canned goods, bottled water, board games, a firearm and ammo was all a family was going to need. (Where are you now, Dreasley? Still sniffing out Reds in the Fort Worth public school system?)

To be fair, it wasn't just Birchers calling for us to dig. President Kennedy had done so too, in a televised address. In our neighborhood, plans for a community shelter took shape—one big shelter to accommodate everybody. Night after night the fathers met in the various living rooms. At one of these gatherings Daddy stood up and raised the question of colored maids. Were they to be left behind when we white folk ran for cover? Daddy alone had thought of this. He pictured Otta Mae washing and ironing as the Bomb bore down on her. "I'm buying places in the shelter for my wife and myself and our two boys. And a fifth spot for Miss Otta Mae Lowe, our beloved employee of many years," Daddy told the crowd, "and when the rest of you have reflected a little, I believe you'll do no less for your own domestic help." A general silence. Was integration going to come to Ranier Court along with the end the world? Daddy came home working his jaw. He told Mom what had happened. He said the matter of the help had been swept aside when someone raised the less vexing question of whether to admit cats and dogs.

Howie Feinberg, my friend from down the street, got the idea that he and I should do our part by establishing where this shelter was to be, so we could start digging. I'd seen photos of the *Queen Mary* in *Life* magazine and envisaged similar saloons and staterooms in our subterranean home away from home. The colored maids could as easily be colored maids down there. What was the problem?

Mom and Dad as I first knew them.

My father was a self-made businessman with no flim-flam about him. He had dead reckoning in money matters and a ready contempt for touts and frauds. And for vacillators: A weak-willed associate was a fart that didn't know which pant leg to run down. And for independent women: A vibrant or fun-loving widow was likely to have poisoned her husband. And for any boy not rough and ready: "Weak handshake. Won't go far." Nor was he modest about his energy and enterprise. "Busy as jumper cables at a Juneteenth picnic!" he liked to say of himself. With maître d's he could be pithy, telling them that the ketchup, at least, had been delicious.

Larky when he had the upper hand, Dad could turn dangerous when thwarted. And he was this way as much at home as in the world. Conditional love was what he had to offer. Perhaps he knew Mom was bestowing on my brother and me the unconditional kind, and thought that hers would do. But to be loved just for being alive is what a child seeks. If not for Mom, Tommy and I would have had to get by on the love we earned: not nearly enough to live on. The sound of her shoes in the front hall was happiness. The sound of his was, often as not, a warning.

I vividly recall the grand opening of a Ramada Inn on which Daddy held the franchise in San Antonio. His guest of honor was a recent Miss Oklahoma, Anita Bryant. I had a case on her and said how much I liked "Paper Roses," included on *Hear Anita Bryant in Your Home Tonight!*, her LP on sale in the lobby, whereupon she took me by the hand and we walked around the motel swimming pool. Anita afterward blazed two paths of glory—as spokeswoman for the Florida Citrus Commission and as the nation's leading opponent of homosexuality.

Our father subscribed to perfection. He liked telling Tommy and me what was wrong with the Christians: They excused themselves on account of original sin, excused themselves and got drunk. (Mom wished he wouldn't instill such prejudices against the majority; we lived among them on sufferance.) But what he was really after was not so much perfection as perfect self-presentation. When among elegant people he talked like them. At home he was ungrammatical. (Mom spoke the same to everybody, everywhere.) In Oxxford suits and Countess Mara ties and smelling lightly of Lilac Vegetal, Dad announced himself faultless. His shirts were custom-made and highly starched. Shaking hands, he shot a monogrammed cuff. At home in undershorts he was big and fleshy, yes. But the contained figure hurrying along West Seventh Street drew looks of admiration and perhaps some curiosity about what the up-and-comer's briefcase held. Only one defect preyed on him: a mouth of gold-filled teeth, hard on a man so vain of his appearance. He'd been told from time to time that he looked like Victor Mature. Then one afternoon Daddy came home from the dentist with Victor Mature's smile—"a complete set of Hollywoods," as he called his new appliances.

The fresh knowledge that followed upon November 22, 1963, was a discovery of history not as what happened in the past but as the current we rode. Until then I'd seen us Taylors as an autarky or closed system. From that day, we braved the elements alongside everyone else. All of humanity attending the same televised funeral was enough to make us know it.

Three events yanked me from the random floating mental life of childhood and propelled me into youth: the fire and the assassination, both of which happened; and midway between these, in October of 1962, the end of the world, which did not. I suppose it was contingency I was discovering in those years, to give it an abstract name. After the fire I understood, in a nine-year-old way, that nothing at all was guaranteed, that we Taylors were the playthings of chance. When my father told me what had happened he hid his face with his hat as he said, very slowly: "Big Bubbe is gone. Barbara is gone. Lisa is gone. Tannie is gone. And Aunt Pesh is very sick." It was the only time he ever let me see him sob.

My emotion, which I remember accurately, was hatred of him for not preventing such things. What he was telling me through tears I'd heard a week earlier on the news. He and Mom and Tommy had rushed to Tyler that morning. I was left behind in Fort Worth in the care of Howie Feinberg's parents. Marlene, Howie's mother, was an anarchic housekeeper who slopped around most of the day in nightgowns. Milt, his father, allowed no talking at meals so he could concentrate on the food, and didn't close the bathroom door when he defecated. In their telephone hutch you might come upon a can of Raid, some old *TV Guides*, a collection of dead batteries and the core of an apple. Their dog, Mags, infested the upholstery with fleas. Stu, Howie's older brother, kept snacks of pizza under his bed that he or Mags would pull out when hungry. In this squalid place, with Mom and Dad and Tommy enduring the worst in Tyler, I received my sexual education. Stu taught Howie and me, in one evening, all the four-letter words I know to this day. And instructed us nine-year-olds in how to perform oral and anal sex on each other. *"Ta da da boom de ay,"* he sang, *"I'll take your pants away! And while you're standing there, I'll take your underwear!*" That Satan, disguised as a Feinberg, wanted to watch us. And did.

Between the fire and the assassination had come that other schooling in contingency: the end of the world. On Monday evening, October 22, 1962, President Kennedy informed us that we faced a grave threat. "I wish to hell it was Ike in there," said my father as we watched the Oval Office address. Kennedy explained, in his outlandish accent, that the Soviets were readying bases in Cuba from which to launch middle-range nuclear missiles (forty-one of them, though this we were not told) each with a thousand-mile range or more and (this, too, we were not told) a destructive power fifty times that of the Hiroshima bomb. Eighteen thousand times the might of Little Boy was aimed at the USA and as an important air force base, Carswell, and a major aircraft manufacturer, Convair, were located in Fort Worth, it was assumed that our city was earmarked for incineration. "I don't see Kennedy as ready for this," said Daddy.

He reiterated our emergency plan, which Civil Defense had instructed every family to have. If not together at the time of the attack we should look for one another at the breakwater of Benbrook Lake. As if I'd have had the slightest clue how to get there. But I do recall a sudden image I got of desperate throngs encamped on the ridge of the dam.

Dad was wrong to doubt Kennedy's adequacy. He'd coolly played for time, postponing the preemptive attack almost everyone around him, in uniform and out, was urging. Such a move—supported by Dean Acheson, Lyndon Johnson, Robert McNamara, McGeorge Bundy and the Joint Chiefs—would have set in motion a sequence of retaliatory strikes and counterstrikes that would have killed tens of millions, poisoned the planet and doomed survivors to a subsistence that did not bear imagining. ("Retaliatory" had been the one word the President stumbled on in his Oval Office address.)

Next day by noon the supermarket shelves were bare. Gasoline hoarders drank the filling stations dry. At school we were ordered to windowless inner rooms and kept there for hours. Mr. Lea, who seemed eager for the coming battle, kept us busy with duck-and-cover drills. The dangerous course of day-to-day events (not least among them, communications through an all-important back channel—a KGB officer who spoke sub rosa for Nikita Khrushchev) was of course known to no one.

On Thursday came Adlai Stevenson's bravura appearance in the General Assembly of the UN: "Do you, Ambassador Zorin, deny that the USSR has placed and is placing medium- and intermediate-range missiles and sites in Cuba? Yes or no? Don't wait for the translation. Yes or no? . . . I am prepared to wait for my answer until hell freezes over."

We got through Saturday, the most dangerous twenty-four hours in human history, not knowing that Khrushchev had followed up a conciliatory letter of the previous day, Friday—proposing withdrawal of the Soviet arsenal if we would pledge never again to invade Cuba and to remove our Jupiter missiles from Turkey—with a hard-line message on Saturday that seemed to make war inevitable. This second letter, so contrary to the first, even aroused suspicion that Khrushchev had been replaced in a palace coup. (In reality, that would come two years later.) Additionally there was the downing of one of our U-2s over Cuba. And in the midst of all this, Kennedy suavely ignored the loss of the reconnaissance pilot and plane, responded constructively to Khrushchev's first letter, ignored his second. . . .

And waited.

Strategic Air Command bombers circled the Arctic that night, prepared to strike targets within the USSR. Other bombers had their instruction packets for a Caribbean assault at daybreak. Our ships were ready to land battalions; they'd have been annihilated; unknown to anyone in Washington, the Soviets had also smuggled short-range battle nukes into Cuba expressly for use against a naval invasion.

Late Saturday evening Attorney General Robert Kennedy met with Soviet ambassador Anatoly Dobrynin. Speaking on the President's authority, RFK agreed, in exchange for withdrawal of all missiles from Cuba, to make no further attempts on the Castro regime. And to remove our missiles from Turkey, provided this remain secret.

At ten o'clock central time that morning, Khrushchev announced the end of the crisis. Mom said so when she picked me up from Sunday school. We took the long way home, through Forest Park. She turned off the radio. "I think this is nice," she said. "Just you and me, driving around. I think this is plenty nice." Embarrassed as always by adult emotion, I nodded. The world, a great glory, looked its old self.

Who in his right mind would have preferred Richard Nixon giving orders during those thirteen days? Unremarked by reviewers of Robert A. Caro's *The Passage of Power*, volume four of his magisterial life of Lyndon Johnson, was a careful analysis of vote tallies from two critical counties of the Rio Grande Valley in the 1960 presidential election. Lyndon Johnson had been brought onto the Democratic ticket to ensure that Texas, which had gone for Eisenhower in the previous two cycles, would come back to the Democrats. Without those twenty-four electoral votes there was simply no path to a Kennedy–Johnson victory.

No polite way to say this: On the evening of the elections, Lyndon's strongman in the Valley, George Parr, the "Duke of Duval County," held back returns till he saw how many votes were needed. (By similar means he and Lyndon had stolen a Senate election twelve years earlier.)

My father used to talk smilingly about the Duke, whom he'd known in the Valley, where as a young man importing Mexican bananas Dad first made a name for himself. "George? Colorful character. Jovial. Ruthless. We heard some pretty bad stories. 'El Jefe' to the Mexicans—Mexican-*Americans*, I mean, but who the hell said that? The Mexicans voted how he told them to. He bought their poll-tax certificates for a buck apiece, which was real money to Mexicans, and delivered their votes to the polling place." That's how politics was done in Duval and Wells and seven other counties, all of them in the Duke's pocket.

I have a fragmentary memory of election night,

1960. I knew the Kennedy campaign song, made famous by Sinatra to the tune of "High Hopes," and stormed around the house singing it: *"Everyone is voting for Jack, 'cause he's got what all the rest lack! Everyone wants to—BACK—JACK! Jack is on the right track!"* High hopes indeed, for what Lyndon and the Duke could bring to pass. Caro's research reveals that in a presidential election decided by forty-six thousand ballots in Texas, the Duke delivered improbable majorities—more than ninety percent in some of the nine precincts—to the Democratic ticket. About fifty-two thousand votes, what was needed plus a little, and Texas went for Kennedy–Johnson.

"Would steal a red-hot stove," was my father's verdict on LBJ, whom he considered a worse scoundrel than the Duke. But forget red-hot stoves. On the night of November 8, 1960, George Parr and Lyndon Johnson, acting together, finagled twenty-four electoral votes for, let us say, the good of the nation. One can't help being grateful that they did.

That autumn Little Bubbe, who was dying of nephritis, had come to stay with us. She observed my Kennedy mania: eight years old and a political animal. "Could be a very disappointed little boy," I remember her saying on election night. But no one need have worried, with Lyndon on the ticket. Were the Kennedys even aware of how much they owed him?

Grandpa Bockstein, a man of very strict routines, would throw back a shot of Crown Royal every day at noon, shudder as if taking medicine and tuck into his lunch, a well-done sirloin and buttered baked potato. (He couldn't bear, at any meal, to see a green vegetable.) My own father's relationship to alcohol was profligate by comparison— one measure of how rapid our acculturation from Polish shtetl to American suburb had been. "Bartender!" he'd call out, meaning me, and order a Chivas and soda, or sometimes a Courvoisier and water. And sometimes he'd send me into the bar to shake a martini. We watched *Huntley-Brinkley* while he drank. I sat on the floor, had done so for years, the way children do, liking the floor. Then one evening he looked at me and said: "What the hell are you doing on the floor? Go sit in a chair." But if I often saw him testy or riled, I never saw him drunk. About the shoal marked alcoholism, on which so many families went aground, we knew nothing.

Reading the renowned memoirs, I'm struck by what extremes they recount. Mary McCarthy's mother and father died of the flu within twenty-four hours of each other when she was six. Mikal Gilmore grew up the younger brother of Gary Gilmore. Kathryn Harrison was her father's lover. Mary Karr's mother came after her with a knife. Lucy Grealy lost a portion of her face to cancer. Alison Bechdel's father threw himself under the wheels of an oncoming truck. David Small's radiologist father treated him for asthma with large doses of X-ray leading to cancer of the larynx. Examples could be multiplied. The things I saw in other homes sometimes made me laugh, as when Milt Feinberg licked the mouth of the ketchup bottle before passing it to me. "Milt!" his wife cried, probably because she saw the look of revulsion on my face. Yes, the Feinbergs' prig of a guest, taken in on a moment's notice, found them uncouth. But what would I have made of things in other homes for which I hadn't even the names? Dysfunction flourished all around yet I was oblivious to it. We lived without any of the curses: no madness, violence, bankruptcy, drug-taking, drunkenness, incest or desertion. Not even an apple core where it shouldn't have been.

As a small child I was a payer of calls throughout the neighborhood. My parents had built the comfortable, unpretentious flagstone house at the crest of the hill two years before I was born. Ranier Court was the only world I knew. Accompanied by Jeff and Davy, my beagles, and armed with social skills that were none of the finest, I'd choose a doorbell and ring it, confident of being brought inside for a cookie and glass of milk while Jeff and Davy dug up the flower beds. The Goulds, the McDonalds, the McCanns, the Salems, the Thompsons, the Suggses, the Stevenses, the Dominys, the

Wests. Some of these households had more melancholy in them than others. One or two were childless and had the deep quiet of childless homes. Each had its own smell and standard of tidiness. In some the good fragrance of beeswax on wooden floors prevailed. In others it was cigarettes and old cooking. And, in not a few, demons crouched at the hearthside, invisible to blithe little me. I was something like Gertrude Flannery, the roving girl in John Cheever's story "The Country Husband": "Opening your front door in the morning, you would find Gertrude on your stoop. Going into the bathroom to shave, you would find Gertrude on the toilet. . . . She was helpful, pervasive, honest, hungry, and loyal. She never went home of her own choice. When the time to go arrived, she was indifferent to all its signs. 'Go home, Gertrude,' people could be heard saying in one house or another, night after night."

A certain residence on Ranier Court was no-go. The widow Crowley lived there with Half-Pint, her malicious dachshund, which we pronounced "dash hound," and dash he could, right for Jeff's and Davy's throats. We gave the Crowley place a wide berth.

On the next hill and too far to visit was the palatial residence of Mr. and Mrs. Arthur I. Ginsburg. Jeannette was a plainspoken, warm, beautiful woman. Her husband, Arthur, was the most pretentious Jew in Fort Worth. In the aftermath of the Missile Crisis he had decreed for himself a mausoleum that could withstand, as he never tired of telling people, anything short of a direct nuclear strike. Friends would be driven to the cemetery to view this rose marble wonder.

Arthur's pomposity was the rack on which Jeannette lived, as my mother used to say. About twenty years ago, when I was home on a visit, Mom looked up one evening from her *Star-Telegram*. "It says here that Arthur Ginsburg has died."

"Are they sure?" said Dad and went back to what he'd been doing. Speak only well of the dead, ancient Rome advised: *De mortuis nil nisi bonum.* As if anybody could adhere to such a ridiculous maxim. My father certainly did not, and made no bones about it. More than once I remember him saying:

"Rabbi's eulogy made me want to open the box and see who was in there."

Now my parents lie together beneath a plain slab of black marble near Arthur I. Ginsburg's magnificent tomb, which casts no shadow on them at any hour of the day.

CHAPTER THREE

THE REAL MAN,
THE IMAGINATION

My best friend was Robby Anton. From him I learned a more whimsical way of life than Taylors or Bocksteins could teach. We thought the funniest thing was to telephone some hotel in the red-light district and attempt, in elevated language, to make a reservation. Or else we'd sit in his mother's Cadillac and be a couple of stars driving from Fort Worth to New York to open in a Broadway show. While others played ball outside, Robby and I would lie around his house or mine listening to Sophie Tucker, last of the red-hot mamas, sing: *"Who wants 'em tall, dark and handsome! Who cares about glamorous guys!"* We loved the great indoors. One Saturday, in a corner of my bedroom, we opened an expensive Polynesian restaurant. On a sleepover at his house, draped in afghans and turbaned in bath towels, we lip-synched highlights from *Lucia di Lammermoor,* seen at the Fort Worth Opera with a senescent Lily Pons in the lead and an unknown twenty-one-year-old Spaniard named Plácido Domingo as her Edgardo. Ordinary boys we were not. We adored theater and ceremony and pomp and pretense of every kind. We especially loved funerals. One time we put on a funeral for a bookmark.

While there has been life for me after Robby, more than thirty years of it, there was none at all before. His parents were the closest friends of mine—you rarely saw Shirley and Charlie without Sol and Annette—and so it happened quite naturally that Robby, three years older than I, became my first friend, a piece of luck I'll marvel at till I die: to have been granted from earliest childhood the company of a creative genius.

My earliest memory of him must be from when I was about five and he eight—an eight-year-old artist in the spell of his calling, which was puppetry. He had a stage his parents had brought back from FAO Schwarz (I wailed till my parents got me one like it), complete with a set of hand puppets: an alligator, a glowworm, a cockatoo, a bearded lady, a heavy-lidded ostrich, a monkey with a scarlet maw and so forth. And how, with his effortless theatricality, Robby stirred them all to life! After a few attempts to emulate him at home on my own bare stage, I folded it up and put it away. Under my tutelage the puppets had refused to live. With glass eyes they reproached me.

Yes, I was a flop—who decided, like flops before me, that reflected glory would be better than none at all. So I made myself Robby's factotum, taking up the slack backstage, operating the lights out front, et cetera. Our audience? Our squirming and benevolent parents, and, occasionally, our guffawing older brothers.

Anything on a stage was rapture. Galvanized by Fort Worth Opera's *Madame Butterfly*, we decided to mount a version of our own and commandeered two girls from Mrs. Westbrook's class, Libby Lee and Angela Tipton, to play Cho-Cho-San and Suzuki. I myself would take the role of Captain Pinkerton.

Libby and Angela were a couple of troupers. They had ballet recitals to their credit and we felt, somehow, that their tutus and tights would look Japanese enough. I'd wear my new seersucker for Pinkerton's regalia. At Record Town we bought the Angel LP set of Victoria de los Ángeles and Jussi Björling singing *Butterfly*. The idea was that Angela, Libby and I would lip-synch the whole thing. Robby painted the flats and put me in charge of staging. Who was going to see this opera? That we'd figure out later.

Angela, a fiery girl, felt miscast as Suzuki and hankered for the starring role. Midway through the dress rehearsal, that hellcat spat on us both. Robby said, "You're gonna get it, girlie!" Libby leapt in. I gave her a hard pinch. Still in their tights and tutus, she and Angela flew out the front door, roller bags clattering behind them. Libby's had a dud wheel, which for some reason made Robby and me laugh uncontrollably.

"Did you see that *wheel*?" he managed to say through tears.

"She *deserves* it!" We fell against each other.

Last we saw, Libby and Angela were waving down some car. Of a nice person, we hoped. More helpless laughter. But our *Butterfly* had perished in the larval stage.

Many years later Robby said: "Pathetic of us to have employed those girls when what we wanted was to be Cho-Cho-San and Suzuki ourselves."

It was with puppets that Robby began and with puppets that he ended. That he became in the last decade of his brief life one of the greatest puppeteers who has ever lived is not doubted by those who saw his work of the late seventies and early eighties. This time he made the protean characters from scratch, a cast of tiny finger puppets who broached the darkness, made alchemical discoveries, suffered and were metamorphosed from their illusions. His theater was a single-handed mythology, outside all creeds and yet systematic. William Blake comes to mind as a comparably uncompromising artist and Blake was among Robby's fascinations. Like the author of *The Marriage of Heaven and Hell*, Robby invented an allegory in which characters embody instincts and faculties. He drew the numinous circle around these human things in order to show, as myth does, how interfused they are with a universe of powers transcending them.

In other words, he had the religious gift (so lacking in rationalistic me). Our journey out of the little world of reason and sense experience and into eternity was Robby's mature subject. Our alleged mortality he saw as a deceit. He would have understood at once what Blake wrote to George Cumberland in April of 1827: "I have been very near the Gates of Death & have returned very weak & an Old Man feeble and tottering, but not in Spirit & Life not in The Real Man The Imagination which Liveth for ever." The fallen world was temporary. The true, ever-living world, all around us but

Robby at work in the Château de Vincennes.

Three of his visionary company.

unseen, a holy secret, revealed itself through mystical experience. Although a marvelous draftsman, Robby had (again in common with Blake) no interest in landscape or in depicting the human form from nature. I see this now as of a piece with his transcendental preoccupations.

The delicious companion of my childhood had become Robert Anton the grown-up puppeteer. Everything the Romantics taught about the momentousness of childhood, about original untutored prowess as the source of art, was borne out in him. What happened is what always happens: Maturity intensified by orders of magnitude the early promptings and intuitions. The cabinet of curiosities from FAO Schwarz gave way to a visionary company of the puppeteer's own making. Twenty-two years ago I tried, in a novel called *Tales Out of School*, to impart something of what this theater was like. Much the most fantastical thing in the book, it's the only part I didn't make up:

"On the planks smoke rose from a tiny cauldron. A couple of bowls—the halves of a robin's egg, really—lay side by side at the foot of a peach tree, two span high, which was coming into flower.

Here was a world of smallness made clear by what it excluded. Simpler than the big world, yes; the big world excludes nothing and this makes the big world hard to see. But here in smallness dwelled the promise of a truth.

"There came a scratching noise from under the platform. The proboscis of a horseshoe crab poked up through the planks. He lumbered on stage doing a side-to-side step. Ah, he wasn't a crab. He was a puppet wearing the carapace of a crab. Now he shed his shell and was a lovely white-faced lady. The proboscis, unwound, became a head of hair which he—no, she—proceeded to comb out with delicate fingers.

"Looking to right and left, she put the peach tree under one arm, climbed into the carapace and sailed away. But here Schmulowicz [the puppeteer] snapped his fingers, summoning her on stage again. He pointed sternly to where the tree had stood. Red in the face, she put it back.

"Schmulowicz now produced a little torch, put it in the lovely lady's hand and, pointing to the footlight candles, bade her light them, which she did. She held the tiny flame back up to him; he blew it out. Then she put the brand, still smoking, under her arm, climbed into the carapace and sailed away. But Schmulowicz snapped his fingers, summoning her back. He put a finger under her dress; she pushed it away. He glowered at her until she complied— hoisting her skirts, squatting, shuddering. At length, she laid an egg into Schmulowicz's waiting palm; and, in great weariness, went back to her carapace, lay down and slept.

"There came a harried headless man on stage— his arms turbulent—rushing this way and that in search of what he lacked. After some groping about, he found the egg in Schmulowicz's hand, fitted it onto his spindle neck and began to bang at it with his fists. Fragments of eggshell fell away, and now a miniature of the head of Schmulowicz himself was discovered. Big Schmulowicz offered little Schmu- lowicz a hand mirror into which little Schmulowicz gazed, not without admiration, picking the last of the eggshell from off his head. He looked and looked, growing vain. Then big Schmulowicz snatched away the looking glass and broke it.

"Now little Schmulowicz rushed over to the

lovely lady, asleep in her shell. Wake up, wake up. He needed for her to admire him, love him, see that he was beautiful. Wake up. She would not. She only turned over. Wake up. Big Schmulowicz intervened, removing little Schmulowicz's head, putting it in his pocket. And that was that.

"The lovely lady turned over, stretched, yawned, arose; but she was no longer lovely. She was a bird of prey, indigo-plumed and with a hooked beak. Her head jerked nervously, as if a quarry were near. Oh, terrible. Then she flew up, perched herself on the crossbeam above the stage—freed (it seemed) of the puppeteer's mastery. But the life was draining out of her from the moment she took wing. She had flown, and where she had flown she stayed: humped on the crossbeam, quite, quite still, because dead now."

They delighted the eye and filled the mind, Robby's homemade creatures, who would turn to the deity who'd made them with love, fear, bafflement, the whole range of feeling.

Shirley and Charlie must have wondered what they'd wrought in this prodigal son. But along with bewilderment there was love, there was money. The hothouse flower was encouraged to bloom. He had pictures to look at, plays and musicals and movies and operas to go to, books to read, records to listen to: the art of Dürer, Blake, Fuseli, Redon, Grosz; the films of Fellini (especially *Juliet of the Spirits* and *Toby Dammit*) and Kubrick (especially *2001*); the writings of Paracelsus, Saint John of the Cross, Jakob Boehme, Meher Baba and C. G. Jung; the songs of Brecht and Weill (especially from *Mahagonny*) and of Cole Porter (especially from *Kiss Me, Kate*). The American musical theater was Robby's Great Code. Expectable in someone of our bent. But "Havana Song" or "Begin the Beguine" or "Another Op'nin', Another Show" interpreted in the light of Paracelsus? That was new. As in childhood, so again in adolescence and beyond: I was his slave, doing my best to wade through Meher Baba, even immersing myself in the mystical puzzles of Jakob Boehme.

Robby's puppets lie orphaned in a trunk and will never be famous. But fame and the sublime are only accidentally related. This we must believe, or

else surrender to a worldliness honoring only success. Robby's immense gifts were known to but a
handful of people and it may be, given his indiffer-
ence to recognition, that he'd have remained a
close-held secret even if allowed to live out a long
life. Once in a while, however, I still meet someone
who actually saw a performance of his. It happens
less and less, of course, and eventually the next-to-
last and last of us who saw the thing will die. For
now, though, we are a happy few, content to have
sat in the long ago before a tiny stage beholding a
stupendous wonder of art.

The long ago: that is to say the sunlit late seventies. Then a cloud settled down on earth to see how
many of us it could devour—the part of the story
everyone knows. Robby was an early case. He fell
ill in the spring of 1983. Watching my adored friend
as the darkness enveloped him, I did not imagine
how many more I'd see vanish in their turn.

That subtraction of wit, grace, brains and beauty
from our midst is unbearable to contemplate. How

is it we did not, in compassionate horror, pull the earth up over us? How is it we who were spared have gone on creating, laughing, renewing ourselves with love? Is the appetite for life simply too great, greater than our accumulated griefs? And what, for their part, do the lost travelers under the hill think of us? Do they applaud our resilience? When I get a moment with them in dreams they tend to say that yes, they do.

George Richmond writes to Samuel Palmer, Blake's disciple: "Just before he died His Countenance became fair. His eyes Brighten'd and he burst out into Singing of the things he saw in Heaven." Justice would have Robby full of years and singing. But Robert Anton died young and alone and humiliated and frightened—and by his own hand, having endured enough—in a Los Angeles hotel room.

They say that coming and going, Palmer would kiss the bell handle of Blake's lodgings. As a boy Robby had a comparably ardent disciple on the threshold at 3912 Ann Arbor Court. My mother would drop me off on Sunday afternoons. After decently greeting his parents, busy with some football game or golf tournament on television, I would make my way to the heaven of art, Robby's bedroom. Here was where the real man, the imagination, lived. Here was where nothing bad could happen. When I dream about him we're there again. Having greeted Shirley and Charlie, I hurry to Robby's room. I find him huddled up, the prodigal come home, sick but hanging on. I say, *You're dead.* He says, *Not for a minute.* I say, *Lo, these many years.* He says, *Illusion.* I say, *The dead are dead.* He says, *Only out of sight.* He asks for news, wants very much to know how everyone's been getting along. I think I'll not go in, only give the bell handle a kiss, next time I dream I'm there.

An old man I loved said: "When we speak of the past, we lie with every breath we take." Well, no. It's nostalgia that lies. Memory certainly arranges, seeks for the story. Memory is aesthetic. But everything in this memoir happened. The sea change has been from persons into language, not from truth into lies. Years ago I memorized four electric lines from Rilke's Ninth Duino Elegy on the hunch I might need them. In English they go like this—

Once for each thing. Just once; no more. And we
    too,
just once. And never again. But to have been
this once, completely, even if only once:
to have been at one with the earth seems beyond
    undoing.

—and nowadays seem the sum of all wisdom. I am trying to say what it has felt like to be me, this unrepeatable alloy of temperament and circumstance, this particle of history. What I tell is over half a century old but everything is still happening and the past is now. I heap up this monument because my family—Annette, Sol, Tommy, Robby too—have vanished and I cannot allow oblivion to own them altogether.

CHAPTER FOUR

PERU

January 1964. I'm helping Mom arrange chairs in the living room around our new color television. A crowd is coming over for a movie and pick-up dinner. Spare ribs, slaw, adult beverages. *Rebel Without a Cause* is on at eight. It's our first convivial evening since the assassination. We need this party, need it as the nation needs the Beatles, suddenly conquering our radios. The guests are mostly Tommy's friends, now of drinking age. Dad has put the hard stuff out of bounds but there's beer and a lightly spiked punch.

My brother is unbelievably handsome. Mom and Dad seem to fear he could get a girl in the family way just by looking at her. They want him safely married. The two of them, exact contemporaries, had wed at twenty-one, the age their elder boy is now. His campaign for bachelor digs has produced a lot of shouting. A randy young bachelorhood is not on the program. In the little world Mom and Dad come from, a son moves out when he weds, not before. The idea being to confine sex to procreation.

The awkward age is behind Tommy now. He'd left college at one point, declaring that he wanted to labor with his hands. Maybe run a filling station, he said. Dad organized a night job for him, working the injection press at a plastics plant. An exhausted Tommy came home each dawn, scrubbed down with Lava soap and collapsed. Poor boy was back in college before long.

Rebel Without a Cause deals, in what must have

seemed hard-hitting fashion, with a threat the young adults in the room are safely past: juvenile delinquency, as the postwar phrase was. Tommy and his friends aspire to banking and brokerage and corporate law, not driving cars over cliffs. The movie must already look quaint to them in 1964, some eight years after its release, but to me it's high tragedy. I erupt when Sal Mineo gets shot—a bawlarama and the old man does not like it, and says so, and hustles me to my room. I think I cried a lot, more than other boys, and recall no shame that I cried. And watching Nicholas Ray's teen opera today, I get what was going on. Sal Mineo keeps a glossy portrait of Alan Ladd in his school locker. I'd seen *Shane* too. And wanted Shane to come back. And dimly knew that Sal and I were from the same bolt of cloth.

That I was not like other boys, those who remember me from back then will attest. A tiptoe walker, a hand-flapper, a ninny under pressure and a shrieker when frightened or angry. A mortification. The diagnostic name later attached to my symptoms was not yet in use. I was just "troubled" and not what my parents had bargained for. They called me the child of their old age. In fact they were thirty-three when I was born, but Mom had lost two babies, both boys, between Tommy and me. Hence the ten-year gap, and I'd have gone the way of those ghostly brothers but for some kind of surgery making it just possible for Mom to carry to term, then be delivered of me by cesarean section.

I once overheard her tell another woman that she knew she was pregnant with me "the next morning"—after intercourse! I figured out in horror—because she felt so ill. And stayed that way till I arrived. "Your mother was in bed for nine solid months. No letup. You can't imagine how heroic she was," Dad said over and over (which was how my father said things). "And once you arrived, nothing was too much. While you napped she'd iron your *shoelaces*." We ought to have been a big family of neatly stair-stepped sons, but the middle was missing and there was time even for the ironing of a baby's shoelaces.

All for what would grow into the dark spot on their lives. When I was six they took me to my first psychiatrist, a Dr. Knopf in Dallas with whom I played checkers. Knopf was a waste of time and money. What I was, I remained. My handwriting was not just bad but demented. I could not grasp arithmetic. I spilled food at every meal. At roller-skating parties I posed a clear and present danger. My obsessive concern was to memorize every-thing; and to make sure that certain objects on the mantel and coffee table were arranged in a way I thought necessary; and to explain, till all tempers were spoiled, why these objects had to be as I ar-ranged them; and to report on what was up in the spice rack; and to name the ingredients of vanilla extract. My fear of firecrackers, of all loud noises, was mortal. I was as scared of a Roman candle or smoke bomb as of a water moccasin. At gatherings of any kind I was baffled by conversation. How did people know what to say? Had they received the script beforehand and memorized it?

I was fully equipped—a boy with asthma, homosexuality and what would later be called Asperger syndrome. I can make no guess about how I struck other children. I believed they were built of pasteboard and glue and only I was real. In the old days this kind of obliviousness was moral disease. Then "Asperger's" came along, a kinder terminology. Only as I entered my thirties did the eponym make it into popular parlance, even as it was beginning to be phased out diagnostically.

And on an analogous schedule I was phasing the syndrome out of me. In adolescence I would learn the art of eye contact and how to modulate my voice; how to make more friends; how to work successfully (sometimes) with others. In college I studied the attractive and the gifted and built myself a Frankenstein monster from the parts I liked best about them—a persona very nearly the opposite of who I was when alone. I learned the language of social interchange better than all but a handful of its native speakers. I even caused several people to fall in love with me. But from then to now, when someone responds, I know I've brought off a confidence trick.

One other Aspie trait was strong and hung on: a literal-mindedness causing me to believe that everyone was telling the truth. In the planetarium scene of *Rebel Without a Cause* the upturned teenage faces grow solemn when the scientist at the controls says: "Man is an episode of little consequence. We will disappear into the blackness of the space from which we came—destroyed, as we began, in a burst of gas and fire. [*Explosive sound effects.*] The heavens are still and cold once more. . . . Man, existing alone, seems himself an episode of little consequence." And I thought he meant pretty soon. And maybe that's what I was crying about, and with cause. We'd only just escaped the end of the world fifteen months earlier at the hands of Nikita Khrushchev. Now the sun was going to swell up and devour us? Childhood was getting too eventful.

As our guests for *Rebel Without a Cause* left that evening, a nice light snow had started to fall. It would come down for the next thirty-six hours and be known as the Great Blizzard of 1964, a record-breaker for Fort Worth at more than twelve inches. About an hour after I fell asleep Daddy shook me awake. "No school tomorrow. We just heard. Let's you and me go for a drive in the snow." I pulled foul-weather gear over my pajamas, got into galoshes, hooked on earmuffs, and we went to the garage. It took us an hour to get thirty yards down the driveway. We lost heart there, abandoned the car and trudged back to the house. Mom was waiting with hot chocolate for me and an ice-cold stare for Dad. I was put into a bath and could hear them arguing. Tommy didn't come out of his room. I wrote my first poem that night, something about the snowfall being like God giving Earth a kiss and Earth kissing God back. It would be published on page one of the superintendent's city-wide bulletin. Copies survive.

Three weeks later the Beatles were on *Ed Sulli-van*. Two weeks after that Cassius Clay ("the Louisville Lip") beat Sonny Liston (briefly a palatable Negro, at least in that matchup) in seven rounds at

Ranier Court after the (so-called) Great Blizzard.

the Miami Beach Convention Hall. The American ride was picking up speed again.

Mom's ailments came not single spies but in battalions. A terrifying memory: overhearing her say to a woman friend, "I doubt I'll make it to forty-five." Pregnancies and childbirths had weakened her. Spinal stenosis, kidney stones and a host of other excruciating illnesses gave her no respite. Encroaching deafness made her shy with strangers. I never knew my mother healthy. She strove for hardihood, but the impersonation of health kept breaking down.

She was a kindly taskmaster. "Straighten up and fly right" was her severest admonition. "Up and at 'em," "Buckle down, Winsoki" or "The days are slipping by" were likelier. On direst occasions she'd say we were driving her to Wichita Falls (where the state asylum was). Now that so many of my days have slipped by, I want to sit quietly and wait upon moments of the past as they briefly surface. I can walk around at will in the extinguished house and talk everything over with my dead. Not to indulge the counterfactual, of course. Down with "if onlys." What's the point of wishing this had happened or that hadn't? Down with all wishing. But nowadays the best of my waking hours are as if in a screening room where episode after episode reveals itself, tactile and verbatim. The following is, as I calculate it, a few months after our *Rebel Without a Cause* evening:

Tommy, a thrower of things when angry, comes home and throws his books against the wall.

"What on earth?" says Mom.

"I bet a hundred dollars and lost," he says. "Playing pool. What's Dad going to do?"

Yes, what? I peeked out from my bedroom door. These dramas with Tommy frightened but also gratified. I, who'd never held a pool cue, was this evening good as gold; fearful of the coming storm, yes, but basking in my virtue too. A hundred dollars sounded to me like a ruinous sum. My moral condemnation was merciless. Tommy had proved himself no better than the deadly juveniles of *Rebel Without a Cause*. Dad would explode into one of his terrible rages—the Monster Mash, we called it.

But no. His response to financial catastrophe was entirely rational. "I won't have it spread around town that you're a welsher." That word was certainly new to me. "I suppose he pretended to have skills no better than your own." A silence, with Tommy probably nodding. "Then started in with the fancy shots. I saw his kind in the Valley. Pool sharks, cardsharps. Must have spotted you the minute you came in. Phone him. Tell him to come right over. If he says no, tell him it's the only way he'll get his money. I won't have you renege on the bet." "Renege," another new word. "We'll settle it tonight. But I want to look this operator in the eye."

I was an earwitness to all that followed. The pool shark arrived almost immediately, was asked into the front hall and presented with a hundred-dollar bill from the roll of hundreds, fastened with a rubber band, that Daddy kept against unforeseen events up to and including nuclear war. He then distilled his loathing into a single sentence: "Never

Tommy in his pool-hall phase.

come near my son again." The pool shark started to answer but Daddy cut him off with a martial "Dis*missed!*"—the only word on which he raised his voice all evening. I have hoped all my life for some occasion on which to bark that at someone, but doubt I'd bring it off so well.

This little melodrama was owed to one on the big screen, *The Hustler*, Robert Rossen's blockbuster of a few years earlier. Tommy had been seduced by Paul Newman as "Fast Eddie" Felson. And not he alone; the whole country saw a revival of interest in pool. New halls opened, among them the one on West Berry where my brother got ensnared. I believe that the very worst episode in father-son relations came a few months later when Dad spotted Tommy's car at the forbidden place and went inside. And brought his firstborn out by the collar.

Tommy's television tastes and mine didn't usually match up. We did, however, agree on what to watch each Thursday evening at eight: *The Twilight*

Zone, individual episodes of which we called Zones. I remember one in particular, "The Shelter," in which a neighborhood of nice people turn into savages when they think the Bomb is heading their way. Everybody wants to break down the door of the one provident homeowner who's equipped his house with a shelter. Turns out the Code Red is a false alarm, but not before all neighbors have behaved so badly that afterward they can't look one another in the face.

Anyhow, Tommy and I loved all Zones. The Wednesday six-thirty slot, though, presented problems in a house with only one working set. My own passion, *The Patty Duke Show*, ran on ABC and Tommy's favorite western, *The Virginian*, on NBC. I was the younger and tended to get my way, so Patty it was. Tommy would taunt and hoot and snort as I watched, declaring that there was no such thing as identical *cousins*, the program's ludicrous premise.

In a photo of my brother at ten holding newborn me up to the camera, he is alight with goodwill. Was any only child ever a better sport about ceasing to be one? Occasionally he'd say: "Make like dandruff, flake off." But mostly he liked taking me along with him. And telling people that both of us were left-handed and wasn't that something? I see now that he wasn't only being good, though good he was. I was a force multiplier. The little sidekick made the dashing lover boy even more attractive. Scores of beautiful girls cooed and fussed and petted my hair.

He was much too large and glamorous to get to know, really, though he lived only one bedroom away. My most urgent question every afternoon when I got home from school was whether he'd be at dinner, as the evening meal was always so much more fun (and unpredictable) when my hero was there. I wasn't his hero, of course. How could I have been, given the age difference? But he did view the two of us as confederates and at difficult moments would talk to me quietly, encouragingly, about better days to come. During one of these quiet talks he said the single most truthful thing about our mother anyone ever said: "She fights the battles we know nothing about."

Myself with chickenpox, as photographed by Tommy.

Tommy died on February 19, 2006, in a snow-mobiling accident at Saranac Lake in upstate New York. My sister-in-law was grievously injured and we did not expect her to survive, though through bravery and fierce will she did. Mom's and Dad's own deaths began that day. I wondered if I was going under too. One night or more, blind with grief, I went to bed hoping not to wake up. A little poem by Langston Hughes ran on a loop through my head:

> *Wave of sorrow,*
> *Do not drown me now:*
>
> *I see the island*
> *Still ahead somehow.*
>
> *I see the island*
> *And its sands are fair:*
>
> *Wave of sorrow,*
> *Take me there.*

All their lives my brother and father had helplessly rubbed each other the wrong way. I recall Tommy shouting in a rage: "One day I won't be known as your son! You'll be known as my father!" And this is what happened, in the world of finance they inhabited. I prefer to think that my brother's life was whole, even if unfinished. What I mean is that everything he meant to do, he did. A realist tends to get the things he dreams of and my brother was one of life's realistic dreamers and one of life's ferocious workers. And now he sleeps on a bluff in Nantucket and can dream whatever he likes, with the whole of the Atlantic for his lookout.

The last time I saw him was a month or two before he died. I was hurrying down Sixth Avenue on an errand. The crowd parted and there he was, in New York for the day, striding up Sixth on an errand of his own. We shook hands, marveling at the coincidence. Anybody would have thought us casual acquaintances. Then we went our separate ways forever.

In the spring of sixth grade Mrs. Westbrook had recommended a hard book to me. I opened it and read the first sentence: "On Friday noon, July the twentieth, 1714, the finest bridge in all Peru broke and precipitated five travelers into the gulf below." Thus I discovered it was possible for a sentence to be a perfect window onto the world. I read on, even with a flashlight after being told to go to bed. The Pocket Books softcover is still with me after all these years and full of my marginalia: "I agree!"—"problems in Lima"—"like Aunt Bess"—"RELIGION"—"Where is Castille?"—and "Am lost here." (In my eleven-year-old mind the Marquesa de Montemayor resembled Great-aunt Bess, who served pimiento-cheese sandwiches and gherkins on her screened porch and told how full her dance card had been back in Shreveport.)

That *The Bridge of San Luis Rey* was a celebrated book I didn't know or need to. Through Thornton Wilder I'd made the vital discovery: that what's really going on in other people—up to then a conundrum—could be intimated in writing. So this was what they called literature. Had those five people really fallen from the hemp bridge into the abyss below? No, but their story was truer than factual truth. Armed with this understanding, I was on my way. I took to calling my bedroom "Peru."

Wilder says about the abbess Madre María del Pilar, who's the heart of wisdom of his book: "Her plain red face had great kindliness, and more idealism than kindliness, and more generalship than idealism." And glimpsing what it felt like to be the harshly dedicated abbess, I wondered about the harshly dedicated Thelma Westbrook, and wondered whether she saw herself in the abbess, and wondered whether I'd known for a moment what it felt like to be one or the other of these stouthearted women. Literature, starting with *The Bridge*, existed to convince me that other people were as real as I was.

That I was unusually privileged to live in a house with a wilderness in the backyard I did not know.

"Down the hill," as we called it, was my other world, my out-of-doors. Down the hill were all manner of flora and fauna. In spring the air was alive with milkweed silk. In early fall the ground would be covered with winged maple seeds. Clouds of gnats came and went. The seventeen-year cicadas burrowed up in the spring of 1964, climbed the trees, burst from their shells, filled the afternoons with chirring and died off six weeks later. A creek bed, usually dry, came fitfully to life after rain and you could strain crawdads and tadpoles from the piddling stream. I brought everything up the hill and into the house: doodle bugs, monarch caterpillars plucked from milkweed plants, the occasional horned frog. At garter snakes Mom drew the line.

Also down there, perched high in a cottonwood, were the bare remains of what had been Tommy's tree house. Before I was born he'd appeared as Pud in the local community theater's production of *On Borrowed Time*. The premise of this melodrama is too silly to explain (and too difficult). Suffice it to say that *On Borrowed Time* is about a preternatural

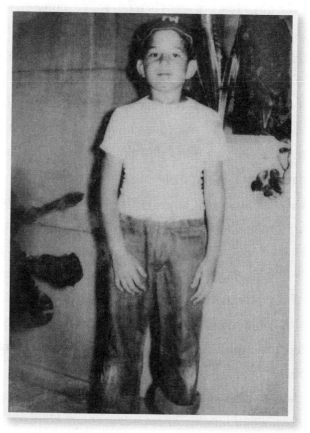

Tommy as Pud Northrup in On Borrowed Time.

tree possessing the power both to kill and to save. At one performance Tommy lost his footing and fell from a low branch when he wasn't supposed to. Instead of crying he began to laugh and had to be shaken by one of the grown-ups onstage. It was a serious play, after all. Was this star turn what had made my daredevil brother want a tree house? He got it, a wonder of professional carpentry with a rope ladder you could pull up after you. That my parents, with their instinctive caution, would have let a harum-scarum boy have such an aerie, and get up to who knew what, and maybe fall—not harmlessly as in *On Borrowed Time*—remains a mystery.

But all that was *in illo tempore*, before the advent of me. Peering into the crown of our cottonwood, all I could see of the now defunct tree house were a few cross-planks. Yet I held fast to the conviction that it would soon be restored and mine. Not a chance. With me Mom and Dad had turned against running such risks. There were enough contingencies down the hill in any case. The occasional bully from another neighborhood, for instance, whom

I'd tell in a quavering voice to get off our land. And then there were the snakes—real ones, not green garters: bull snakes, which one needn't fear, but once in a great while a water moccasin, copperhead or rattler. "Fifty-footers" these were called, meaning that fifty feet was as far as you got after one of them bit you. They mostly ate the rodent life and slept in the sun, but a lethal bite could have been my fate. I knew the story of a Fort Worth boy, a contemporary of Tommy's, who'd been struck in the face by a diamondback and died.

Among my parents' favorite friends were Lou and Dorothy Metzinger, whom we visited whenever in Houston. Their home was a citadel of high culture and their three children were exemplary: Susan, the beautiful and brilliant eldest; Anita, a classic middle child, happy to have made the team; and Danny, the apple of the eye, with whom I always had such good fun.

Too good in the end. Danny had come to stay

with us for a few days in the summer of 1963, about the time I turned eleven. All was going so well. An outing to the Botanic Garden, which we in Fort Worth imagined to be exceptional although it was not. An afternoon at the Amon Carter Museum with its collection of western art. (A little of Frederic Remington and Charles Russell went a long way with me even then.) A Saturday-evening performance of *West Side Story* at Casa Mañana, our mostly professional summer stock theater.

"No substitute for exposure" was the old man's motto. Taking it to heart in my bedroom once the lights were out, I slipped out of my pajama bottoms and instructed beautiful, perfect Danny to remove his too. After only a few minutes of ecstatic fumbling the lights were on and there Dad stood, glowering and gigantic in the doorway. He ordered Danny first to the living room for interrogation, then me. After I'd admitted in anatomical detail to every deed, he told me that Danny insisted we'd done nothing wrong at all. God damn me, I'd ratted us out.

Next day, when the Metzingers arrived to pick

Danny up, Dad behaved as if all were well; but I could see that his brow stayed knitted. Danny and I were involved in some sort of board game on the living room floor. Suddenly I stood up in a towering rage and shouted, *"Cheater! Cheater!"* The term "meltdown," not yet standard, would have covered it. I was ordered to Peru, then ordered back five minutes later to say good-bye to the Metzingers. Knowing his son was blameless, Lou Metzinger tossed over his shoulder as they left: "Come visit us cheaters in Houston sometime." I can imagine Danny saying as they sped away: "Please don't leave me with those awful people anymore." And Lou saying: "Don't you worry about *that*, son." Relations between the Metzingers and my parents were never the same. And it was my fault.

Several years later I did see Danny again. By then we were teenagers, he very graceful and I— something else. "Remember that time you got so mad at me?" he asked with the best will in the world. And given my chance to apologize, I added fresh dishonor to old outrage by saying I had no idea what he was talking about.

Many years after that, by which time Danny and I were middle-aged men, and other people's troubles were finally telling a little on my selfish heart, came the news that his older sister, Susan, who'd read a one-act play I wrote at fifteen and offered constructive criticism and told me I had talent—that Susan had killed herself. And that a few years later Mr. Metzinger, who'd dealt with me as I deserved on the day of my horrible conduct—that Mr. Metzinger had shipped on a tramp steamer, died in unexplained circumstances and been buried at sea.

Now I've concluded middle age. How do I know, apart from the reckoning of years? Because what has vanished is so much more substantial than what is present. If I appear half absent to friends, it's that I'm extremely active somewhere else—call it Peru—and in a terrible state of love for a world blown away like smoke and ash but to which I have the most precise and intimate access. "There is a land of the living," Wilder writes at the end of *The Bridge*, "and a land of the dead and the bridge is love, the only survival, the only meaning." On the day I vanish, down comes my bridge, down come my loves, unless I make words span durably where these mirages of memory waver and fade and are gone.

Our parents, upon their engagement.

CHAPTER FIVE

FOREBEARS

How different was Mom's family from Dad's! The Bocksteins, so musical, dressy, pleasure-loving and spendthrift. The Taylors, grim as Plymouth Brethren. Harry and Lena Bockstein's Spanish colonial house on Windsor Place always smelled of baking pies. B.B. and Bertha Taylor's house in Tyler smelled of Lysol. The Bocksteins were successful wholesalers of fruits and vegetables and, after the war, frozen foods, as well as distributors of Pearl beer, a premium brand of the time. They had works of art on the walls and went around in a Pierce-Arrow and had live-in servants. The Taylors ran a sad-sack grocery.

Mom's people—the Bocksteins and, on Little Bubbe's side, the Goldbergs—had settled in Fort Worth and Shreveport, respectively, in 1904 and 1907, their passage from the Pale of Settlement paid by Jacob Schiff. This greatest of German Jewish philanthropists was alarmed by the glut of Yiddish speakers in New York and wanted to divert some of the floodtide of immigrants fleeing Poland, Belarus and other imperial Russian lands in the wake of pogroms—at Kishinev, Odessa and Białystok, to name the best-known among hundreds. Schiff's Galveston Movement was based on the idea that Jews landing well away from the Northeast would found new communities of their own in the South and Middle West. This was how my grandparents and great-grandparents came to make new lives in such un-Jewish places. Bubbe Bockstein, née Goldberg, was born in 1896 in Pruzhany, a market town, then Russian, later Polish and now Belarusian, at the confluence of the

Grandpa Bockstein and Little Bubbe.

Big Bubbe and Grandpa Taylor.

Mukha River and the Vets Canal. Grandpa Bockstein, whom she would meet in Shreveport, had been born in 1886 and grew up in Sielce, forty kilometers northwest of Lublin.

Dad's people, also beneficiaries of the Schiff munificence, were from the Podlaski region of northeast Poland. His father, Beshka Treszczanski—who in South Texas promptly became Bob Benjamin Taylor—was from Goniądz, a little town northwest of Białystok. Brainka Rutsky, whom he'd married prior to their departure in 1913—and who in Texas became Bertha Roosth Taylor, destined to perish with three of her granddaughters in the house fire of October of 1961—was from Korycin, two villages away.

Bubbe Taylor's parents, Tanchum Mayer Rutsky and Esther Kowalska Rutsky, had accompanied their daughter and new son-in-law to East Texas in 1913. (It was for Tanchum Mayer Rutsky that my brother, Thomas Malcolm Taylor, was named.) Bubbe Bockstein's parents, Josef Goldberg and Celia Tzina Goldberg, née Bremmer, had settled in 1907 with their children in Shreveport. And a generation before them in northeastern Poland had lived Halel Treszczanski and Shlomo Rutsky, paternal great-great-grandfathers of mine, never in America and about whom I know nothing but their names.

Our ancestors' lives in northeastern Poland and western Belarus were on old stones dating to the fifteenth century. We may have been as ancient there as Yiddish itself, a language my brother and I were the first generation in twenty not to speak. For five hundred years northeastern Poland and southwestern Belarus had been our home, replaced in the nick of time by northeast Texas and western Louisiana, else there would have been no Bocksteins, Goldbergs, Rutskys or Treszczanskis, for the Jews left behind in Sielce, Pruzhany, Korycin and Goniądz were either taken to the edge of town and slaughtered by *Einsatzgruppen* or sent to the gas chambers of Treblinka and Auschwitz. Remembered for a blessing here are Yossel Treszczanski; his wife, Chaya Kowalska Treszczanski; and their children, Rochel, Avrum, Maische and Yentl, my father's second cousins. These were Treszczanskis who did not become Taylors.

Indeed, no fewer than sixty-four Treszczanskis of Goniądz vanished into the Polish abyss that coincided with our American idyll.

I know these names now because of databases and genealogical websites that my parents and grandparents could not have dreamed of. Dad only guessed at the proper spelling of Treszczanski. "Trashansky" was the version he would now and then search for in various North American phone directories. Cold-calling these strangers tended not to produce much, or even go well. "Must have thought I wanted money," he said about a Trashansky in Brooklyn who'd hung up on him.

"I don't think they're even in the United States," he concluded. "I think they're in South America."

Thus was launched the family legend that we had relatives in Rio or Buenos Aires or Caracas. Best not to disturb them down there. We gave the Trashanskys no more thought. But nowadays comes this recurrent dream: I am in the street with friends. We are laughing. My cell phone rings. It is Dad, who says humbly, apologetically, "I know I'm dead. I just want to hear your voice again." Armed with knowledge taken from the Yad Vashem database, I say accusingly, heartlessly, "Ever hear of a place called Goniądz? It's your hometown." I am pitiless. What the hell is wrong with me?

"The Trashanskys—"

"Can't hear you, son, you're breaking up."

"The Trashanskys. Treszczanskis. I've found them." But then I am flooded with shame for thinking I have something to tell him, or any of the dead.

"You were right, Daddy. South America."

But I've lost the connection.

M̲y mother's parents had sponsored a refugee Jewish girl in the spring of 1938, Erika Meyer, who came from Langenfeld, a Rhineland town midway between Cologne and Düsseldorf. She stepped off the train in Fort Worth with five shaky words of English: "I glad to be here." A *Star-Telegram* reporter and photographer were on hand to record the occasion. Bubbe and Grandpa promptly immersed her in the public school system and all aspects of Fort Worth's Jewish community.

It was on CBS Radio that they'd heard Eddie Cantor's appeal to American Jewish families willing to take in refugee children. Bubbe said to Grandpa, "Here's this big house," and contacted the German Children's Jewish Aid. Several months later they were greeting their new charge at the Texas & Pacific depot. Erika was brave, good-looking, witty, popular—and hell-bent on Americanizing herself. There were slumber parties, picture shows, new hairdos taken from the magazines, even new personas. After seeing *The Mark of Zorro* she came home with a faraway look and said her new name was Linda Darnell.

Bubbe and Grandpa didn't adopt her, of course. The idea was that Erika's parents, Bernard and Emmy Meyer, and younger sister, Helga, would come to America as soon as they could. Erika wrote home faithfully to Langenfeld, sending photos and trinkets and newspaper clippings. Then, suddenly, her letters went unanswered. She never heard from her family again. After the war she learned that they had been deported to their deaths at Stutthof concentration camp, east of Danzig.

In the 1980s, in one of those improbable codas sometimes attaching to these stories, Erika very reluctantly went back to Langenfeld and presented herself at the doorstep of Hauptstrasse 133, where she'd lived as a girl. The inhabitants asked her in. They were very glad to see her, as a few years earlier they'd uprooted an old tree in the front lawn and found at the root a strongbox containing letters and photos and news items and mementos from a place called Fort Worth: pictures of the Bocksteins at home; my parents' wedding announcement; pressed corsages. All of this the Meyers had buried, expecting to return.

My deeper suspicion about the Taylors and the Bocksteins is that they had an American determination to be uninjured, unhumiliated, as if the Shoah had happened only to Jews unlike us—Big Max and Little Abeleh, for example, custodians at the synagogue with tattooed numbers on their forearms. The American playwright and critic Lionel Abel wrote that after his mother saw the first newsreel images of the liberated camps she said: "I don't think the Jews can ever get over the disgrace of this." Looking back now, I'm bound to admit that by neither word nor deed did any Bockstein or Taylor try to find out who of our own blood were among the Six Million. Erika's murdered family represented the calamity for us and our curiosity ended with them.

And yet I recently came upon a letter my maternal grandfather wrote in the spring of 1944 to a man in Chicago he believed to be his cousin, in which Grandpa says he hasn't heard from any family in Wolkowysk, his mother Masha Grodzensky Bockstein's birthplace in southwestern Belarus, since 1904. (She'd died in Fort Worth in 1934.) Though the unimaginable extent of Germany's war against the Jews would not be known for another year, this letter can have been prompted only by the growing anxiety he felt. One read by then of systematic exterminations, if not of death camps. Grandpa wrote: "My mother, may she rest in peace, had two sisters, Schala and Davera, and one brother, Yankel," all left behind when she married and moved to Sielce (which my grandfather calls

Siltz). Schala, I now know, came to America with her husband, Shimon Samoschzianski, where they Anglicized their name to Senor. But about Davera and Yankel I can learn nothing at all. Grodzensky is not a common family name and Yad Vashem lists six Grodzenskys of Wolkowysk—three without first names—who were exterminated at Treblinka.

A customized forty-five-rpm record, made in the fifties and long ago gone to smash, carried on one side my brother delivering his bar-mitzvah speech and on the other Little Bubbe singing, in a shaky contralto, "For All We Know," a J. Fred Coots–Sam Lewis hit of the mid-thirties, but with Lewis's lyrics rewritten to express Jewish uncertainty in the Promised Land, shading even into fears that what happened elsewhere could happen here. Where the original song says, "We won't say good-bye until the last minute, I'll hold out my hand and my heart will be in it," our Bubbe sang, "America's clasping her hands, there's a limit. We'll open our shul and we'll find *police* in it—for all we know!"

Congregation Ahavath Shalom. How I dreaded that sepulchral place. After seven hours of school, when I'd have liked to be outdoors exploring nature or indoors exploring topics of my own choosing, I was condemned to Hebrew school. The teachers were a hapless couple, a Mr. and Mrs. Zipper, survivors of Nazism whose appearance, lackluster hygiene, hilarious name, foreign speech and sulfuric rages were our only fun as we watched the sun go down on another lost afternoon. I certainly wasn't there because Mom and Dad were devout. What they were trying to do was appease our forebears from Wolkowysk, Sielce, Pruzhany, Korycin and Goniądz. For them, the sanctified dead, I was offered up, two afternoons a week and twice more on Saturday and Sunday mornings, to Simon and Miriam Zipper.

The good boy vanished when I got to Ahavath Shalom and in his place stood an imp of the perverse. One afternoon, just to see what would happen, I wickedly informed Mrs. Zipper that I was uncircumcised. She shook with rage and reported me to the rabbi. What I'd said was nonsense, of course, though there was an *irregularity* attaching to my circumcision. At

Harris Hospital, when I was three days old, I got mixed in with the gentile baby boys and was modified alongside them. So when I was eight days old, at what ought to have been my bris, there was no foreskin to remove. On the strength of this hospital error I felt I could be Jewish or not as the mood took me.

We ate no catfish. Of the noble structure of Jewish dietary law this single prohibition was all that remained. Mom never mentioned God at all and Dad only by way of imprecation. They forsook the Conservative rite and went over to the Reform. As for Orthodox Jews, Dad couldn't stand them: "The bigger the tallis, the bigger the thief," he used to say. Of my final attendance at High Holy Days with the two of them I chiefly remember what Mom, looking around in amazement, said for all to hear: "I'm not coming back till the whole congregation goes on a diet." Had life been long enough my parents would have continued on to the Unitarians.

Still, I think my Hebrew schooling made them feel better about how ham- and lobster-infested their lives had become. And made me devoutly antireligious. I'd compose my face into an obedient mask while saying inwardly, "There is no God, there is no God," till the bell rang and I could go home. The sanctity of atheism has stayed with me to this day. I hope to die in the odor of it.

When my father graduated from high school his uncle Sam Roosth, Big Bubbe's elder brother, a rough customer who had struck oil in East Texas and who dispensed the family largess and in whose shadow everyone lived, said: "Son, your future's planned. I'm sending you to college and afterward to law school."

My father, who'd always hated school and done poorly there, said: "Uncle Sam, I want to get into business right away." Uncle Sam said nothing. But a day later Dad got from him a graduation gift that said it all. One dollar.

Perhaps inevitably, he formed the ambition that my brother and I should be lawyers, and gave Tommy a copy of *The Story of My Life* by Clarence Darrow. My brother never liked being told by anyone, least of all our father, what he ought to do. He tossed the book aside for me. I was drawn to a particular case, that of Richard Loeb and Nathan Leopold, very wealthy sons of Chicago's Jewish upper crust who in May of 1924, for the pleasure of planning and executing a perfect crime and thereby proving themselves Nietzschean supermen, murdered fourteen-year-old Bobby Franks, a boy from their elegant neighborhood. After bludgeoning him with a chisel and asphyxiating him with a rag, they stripped the child, poured hydrochloric acid on his face and genitals, stuffed him into the drainage pipe of a culvert and sent a ransom note to the frantic parents.

The body was promptly found, along with a pair of eyeglasses. At the funeral parlor these sat on the boy's disfigured face until Mr. and Mrs. Franks said that Bobby wore no glasses. It was then that they became the first and most crucial piece of evidence in the case. The frames themselves were ordinary enough, as was the prescription. But they had an unusual hinge. Only three such pairs had been sold in the Chicago area, two to individuals readily cleared of any possible involvement and the third to Nathan Leopold.

Solving the perfect crime took the state's attorney less than two weeks. Getting the perpetrators to confess took an afternoon and an evening. Leopold had stonewalled, the way Danny Metzinger did with Dad, but Loeb was like me and spilled his guts in a hurry. Before long, both were proudly sharing details of their supermannish deed with prosecutors.

On our bookshelves we had Meyer Levin's *Compulsion*, a true-life novel based on the case. And the four of us had watched on TV the 1959 movie version with Orson Welles as the Clarence Darrow figure, E. G. Marshall as the state's attorney, and Bradford Dillman and Dean Stockwell as the murderers. Like everyone of their generation, my parents were aware of this "crime of the century" with its motiveless malignity and trappings of German Jewish wealth, and were initially amused by my researches. But then, as the obsession took wing, my questions became too many and too unpleasant. I was as roused as if the year were 1924 and the place Cook County. I made my own map of the South Side and environs. X marked the spot where Loeb and Leopold had enticed Bobby into a rented car and another X indicated where they disposed of his body. Over here was where they'd hidden the chisel.

I elaborated a timeline on an adding-machine roll and included stirring words from the great Darrow's closing remarks to the court: "Before I would tie a noose around the neck of a boy, I would try to call back into my mind the emotions of youth. I would try to remember what the world looked like to me when I was a child. . . . The brain of the child is the home of dreams, of castles, of visions, of illusions and of delusions . . . and whether they take one shape or another shape depends not upon the dreamy boy but on what surrounds him."

Part of me, with Darrow, was ready to affirm that nurture was all. The Leopold and Loeb homes must have engendered these monsters. But maybe there was something fatal on the nature side too. An unnamable miasma hung over "Babe" Leopold and "Dickie" Loeb, as they were known, unnamable by me then but soon to be named, and those two psychopaths were the least favorable introduction to grown-up homosexuality that chance could have thrown my way. In a flash I understood that I was their kin, shared their nature and was capable of anything.

CHAPTER SIX

NATURAL SHOCKS

I found a lump in my upper arm and it kept getting bigger. In the spring of 1964 Dr. Fred Aurin, a general surgeon, had checked me into Fort Worth Children's Hospital and taken the tumor out. My parents told me it was benign; but what Dr. Aurin had told them was that it was a rhabdomyosarcoma. I might be losing an arm before long, or my life.

Was this their rationale for the grand trip to New York we took that summer? Rooms at the Plaza overlooking Central Park. Dinners at the

Colony and '21' and La Caravelle and Parioli Romanissimo and the Cub Room of Sherman Billingsley's Stork Club. Midnight snacks in the Palm Court. We were hicks all right but living the life. And I may or may not have been very ill.

Robby and his parents were over at the Regency, having a glamorous time of their own. When I boasted that I'd ridden in an elevator with Lucille Ball, he stared back mildly and told me who was staying at *their* hotel. Richard Burton and Elizabeth Taylor. Said he saw them every day. Said they'd actually said hello.

Burton was starring that year in *Hamlet*, a barebones production performed in (carefully selected) rehearsal clothes under John Gielgud's direction. What scenery there was, Burton ably chewed. A film of the production survives and you can see for yourself. It was my first Shakespeare and his Hamlet remains for me the prototype. At intermission in the lobby of the Lunt-Fontanne we bought an LP record of highlights from the play and for the next few months I flung myself, Burton style, around the living room, crying out with him about the thousand natural shocks flesh is heir to until Tommy said: "You can't do that accent, so stop trying."

We went to the theater nearly every night that June, as my old collection of *Playbills* attests. It was a signal time for Broadway musicals and we saw our share: *A Funny Thing Happened on the Way to the Forum*; *Oliver!*; *110 in the Shade*; *Hello, Dolly!*; *What Makes Sammy Run?*; *Fade Out—Fade In*; *Funny Girl*. Plays too—"the legitimate theater," as Dad loved calling it. My parents were indiscriminate theatergoers, afraid they might miss something. This got transmitted.

Most powerful of all was James Baldwin's *Blues for Mister Charlie*. I had no vocabulary or frame of reference at eleven for what I was seeing and though raised in the South had never heard "nigger," a word regarded with the utmost contempt in our household, flung around as it was on the stage of the ANTA Theatre that night. (I do recall having come home from Mrs. Pakston's kindergarten with the standard counting rhyme—"Eeny meeny miny moe, catch a nigger by the toe"—and being angrily told to say catch a monkey or a spider or anything but a nigger because only trash said "nigger." "Colored" and "Negro" were the respectable words in our Jim Crow universe.)

My visual memory of Baldwin's play is concentrated into a single dramatic moment: Pat Hingle, a powerhouse of the day, telling how his first love had been a girl "the color of gingerbread when it's just come out of the oven" and what had happened when the girl's mother discovered them together. This had the real pity and terror in it. Baldwin had used the horrific martyrdom of Emmett Till, which launched the mid-century civil rights movement, as loose inspiration. *Blues* is about the racially motivated murder of a black man who has gone home to the South after living in Chicago. At the climax the culprit is acquitted, like Till's murderers, by an all-white jury.

Two years before my parents were born, a white vigilante mob of three thousand killed perhaps as many as two hundred blacks in East Saint Louis, Illinois. In the year of my parents' birth, 1919, the most terrible episode of American violence against blacks occurred in and around Elaine, Arkansas, when as many as eight hundred men, women and children were slaughtered by lynch mobs ravening through the Delta. In 1921 the entire Greenwood district of Tulsa was burned down and two hundred or more black residents massacred and ten thousand left homeless.

My parents' native ground, East Texas and West Louisiana, was also very notable for lynchings that mobs carried out with impunity. Tyler or Shreveport could have been the setting for Baldwin's play. In Tyler, one year before the Treszczanskis settled there and became Taylors, a black man named Dan Davis was burned at the stake with unseasoned firewood. A crowd of two thousand attended. That was 1912. In Shreveport lynchings were a way of life: Isaac Pizer in 1896, Jennis Sturs in 1903, Henry Rachel in 1909, Thomas Miles in 1912, Edward Hamilton and Watkins Lewis in 1914, Henry Brooks in 1917.

The Taylors, Roosths, Goldbergs and Bocksteins had lived at close quarters with these horrors. Wherever the influence of the Klan was strong, race hatred shaded over into ethnic and religious hatreds. More than once as a boy my father had been pelted with rocks and called "Christ killer."

At *Blues for Mister Charlie*, as on other theatrical

occasions, I felt misgivings pass between my parents. Should they have taken me along? But they always took me along. In Fort Worth they'd taken me along to see Sally Rand's fan dance. (The one exception had been two years earlier in Las Vegas when they went to something called the Folies Bergère—Folies Brassiere, I thought they'd said. An image arose of statuesque ladies cavorting in plain white bras like Mom's. We were staying at the Desert Inn. An on-staff babysitter, devout enough to carry a Bible in her handbag, had looked after me that evening. I remember how she got lost in her devotions, then popped her head up to say, "Let's look at TV!" as if she'd found the idea in Scripture.)

On summer nights my parents liked taking me to the drive-in. While they watched *Blackboard Jungle*, my first movie (I was three) or, that same year, *The Man with the Golden Arm*, my second, I slept on the backseat under an afghan knitted by Little Bubbe. When I was ten they'd taken me to see Katharine Hepburn and Ralph Richardson in *Long Day's Journey into Night*, also at the drive-in, for which I stayed awake. The one visual memory I have is of a morphine-addled Hepburn when she howls, with a smashing of crockery, *"I hate doctors!"* Beset by dope addiction, alcoholism and tuberculosis, the Tyrone family was not a tribe I could recognize, familiar though the configuration was: mother, father and two boys with a big age gap. The Tyrones had torments bred in the bone. We'd merely suffered a calamity. They were the luckless version of ourselves, who we'd have been if doomed by trouble, which we were not. Everybody who's seen O'Neill's play remembers the impersonation of family happiness that they manage to sustain for the first five minutes. Reflecting on my own family story now that it's over—which was what O'Neill was doing when he wrote his "play of old sorrow, written in tears and blood"—what impresses me is how unbowed my mother and father were, how fit for life, how flinty, even, how determined to get more than the usual five minutes.

Our New York theatergoing in 1964 was overhung by a recent embarrassment. A couple of Broadway producers had ventured as far as Fort Worth in search of backers for a musical life of Sophie Tucker, with music and lyrics by Steve Allen and starring an actress slated for megastardom, Libi Staiger. Like my own parents, Robby's had been lured in. It was how he and I came to be so interested in Sophie. Given that she'd been the biggest entertainer of her day, given that she was still alive to promote the show, given Steve Allen, Mom and Dad thought they couldn't lose. They were longing for a taste of the big time. A cousin of Mom's in Dallas lived off the proceeds of her little stake in *The Music Man*. Why shouldn't such a thing happen to us?

Sophie opened and closed at the Winter Garden in one week. It has the distinction of being not just a bomb but a preeminent bomb. (At Joe Allen's restaurant on West Forty-sixth, where posters of such costly disasters line the walls, *Sophie* has pride of place.) One year later a musical about another homely girl in vaudeville, starring another young woman slated for megastardom, rang all the bells and made its investors very rich. The night we saw Barbra Streisand in *Funny Girl* at the Winter Garden, Mom and Dad were finally laughing about having put their money on the wrong Ziegfeld sensation. But when, a few months later, those same producers approached the folks about a new show—based on the life of ill-fated film star Roscoe "Fatty" Arbuckle, whose trial for the wrongful death of a tootsie had riveted America—Dad hit the ceiling. "What next?" he bellowed. "A musical about Adolf Hitler?" We never touched show business again.

One sweltering afternoon stands out as vividly as any matinee or evening performance: Dad took me to see the old Penn Station, on which demolition had begun some months earlier. This was before the age of implosion. Buildings of such size were dismantled over the course of months or years.

What vindictive hand or eye dared frame the subterranean mess that was going to replace it? The great architectural historian Vincent Scully used to tell his students at Yale that whereas you strode into the old soaring light-filled Penn Station like a prince, you nowadays scurried through the new one like a rat. Those wanting to see the wondrous place as it was can do no better than watch certain movies. In *The Seven Year Itch*, Tom Ewell packs his wife and son off to Maine from there. In *The Palm Beach Story*, Claudette Colbert grabs the train to Florida for a quickie divorce. Best of all for Penn Station admirers is Hitchcock's *Strangers on a Train*, in which you get a real grasp of the lost building's noble concourses and coffered vaults.

How my father loved whistling on two fingers for a taxi, as he did that day at Thirty-first and Eighth. How he loved surprising Jewish cabdrivers— a lot of them still were at the time—by switching from drawling East Texan to idiomatic Yiddish. The romance of New York was strong in Dad and he would sometimes muse on a metropolitan life for us. More practically, he thought he'd have better opportunities if we moved north. A powerful man on Wall Street, Joseph S. Gruss, had taken us under his wing. After Tommy's brief stint on the night shift of that plastics plant, he was in no time a summer apprentice at Mr. Gruss's investment firm on Broad Street and living in the Navarro, a residential hotel on Central Park South. What a transformation! The old bar of Lava soap, six months later, wasn't even worth remembering. And I think it may have been on Mr. Gruss's recommendation that Dad took one of the few real financial risks of his life, a large position in Communications Satellite Corporation on its initial public offering. The company's stock price, like the products it made, went into outer space.

Was it on account of this, rather than my rhabdomyosarcoma, that our suite at the Plaza gave onto Central Park and we dined at '21' and the Colony? Along with the keys, change, pillbox and penknife jingling in his pocket, Dad held there our bright future. "Sol Taylor, from Fort Worth, Texas!" he'd say, putting out his hand to everyone, even to Joe Louis, whom we spotted on Madison Avenue: "Meet my boy, Joe! Son, meet the Champ!" From June 2, the day of our arrival, COMSAT, as the company was called, began trading on the New York Stock Exchange. Daddy was cock of the walk that month and showed me New York as if he owned the place. Because I was sick. Because we were in the chips.

His position in COMSAT amounted to a fraction

of one percent of the company, about half a million 1964 dollars. The stock shot up and split, up and split, up and split once more. I lived from that time with the assurance of money, which made me ignorant of where it came from and reckless in my use of it. "How's about I give you your inheritance in loose bills?" Dad proposed when I went away to school. "That way you can throw it from the rear platform of the train."

I believe the master plan I worked out in those weeks—as mesmerized then by the future as I now am by the past—was that I'd make good on my father's pipe dream and come back to Manhattan to stay. And as a man that's what I did, with, alas, no better idea of the value of a dollar than I'd possessed eating bouillabaisse at the Cub Room in 1964.

The one place I *had* known "nigger" to be flung around was in the pages of *The Adventures of Huckleberry Finn*, recommended by Mrs. Westbrook. It was the summer reading I'd brought to New York.

Having come through the explosion of a steamboat boiler, Huck is fawned over by Aunt Sally. "Good gracious!" she says. "Anybody hurt?"

"No'm," says Huck. "Killed a nigger."

"Well, it's lucky," says Aunt Sally, "because sometimes people do get hurt."

That most violent of American words is scrawled all over our history. Huckleberry, as good a boy as any of us will ever know, has no way not to use it. In the sharecropping Texas and Louisiana my great-grandparents and grandparents immigrated to, it was as universal and unquestioned as it had been in the antebellum Missouri of Mark Twain's boyhood. Nor is it going anywhere. "Antimacassar" and "furbelow" may have fallen out of use, but "nigger" will not. It is invasively rooted in the civilization that gave rise to it and will flourish till the end.

Lionel Trilling, my teacher at Columbia in 1975, the year of his death, wrote this about *Huck*: "To read it young is like planting a tree young—each year adds a new growth year of meaning, and the book is as little likely as the tree to become dull. So, we may imagine, an Athenian boy grew up together with the *Odyssey*. There are few other books which we can know so young and love so long." What struck me most at eleven, and stayed with me longest, and for reasons not far to seek, was the episode in which, for a bit of fun, Huck leaves a dead rattlesnake on Jim's pallet. By the time Jim comes to bed, the dead rattler's mate has arrived and bites him on the heel. Jim instructs Huck, who has promptly killed the second snake, to cut off its head, skin it and roast a piece of the meat, which Jim eats as a homeopathic measure. While his foot and leg balloon with venom, Jim drinks himself delirious from Pap Finn's jug. Only after four days and nights does the danger pass. Then Huck and Jim head downriver on their island of safety, their talismanic raft. "The fifth night we passed St. Louis, and it was like the whole world lit up."

Jim never knows Huck has put the dead snake on that blanket. I think what captivated me was Huck's private guilt, for I was a connoisseur of the emotion. It felt so good to be able to feel bad. "Look me in the eye!" my father would rage when trying to pry this or that confession from me. But my undiscovered trespasses were my treasure: venial bad acts a little; fantasized murders—spotless and undetectable—a lot. Everyone in Fort Worth ought to have feared for his life. At twelve I dreamed up mayhem in order to feel guilty, which in turn made me feel good. And took things to their logical conclusion. Everything was somehow my fault. Reading a few years ago that Alma Mahler believed she was responsible for the First World War, I understood completely. Such comprehensive guilt must have been what it took to cheer her up.

We waited that summer in brutally long lines for the World's Fair pavilions, tacky public-relations monuments to Westinghouse, Pepsi-Cola, General Motors, US Steel, Chunky candy bars, Johnson Wax, IBM, Eastman Kodak, RCA and so on. Did I care? I was not in Flushing Meadows but on a raft with Nigger Jim, reveling with Huck in his bad conscience. After all, he's assisting a runaway slave, Miss Watson's property. Jim says that once he gets to Cairo, Illinois, and is free he's going to save up and buy his wife and two children. And if he can't buy them he's going to get an abolitionist to steal them. "It most froze me to hear such talk," says

Huck; but he concludes, on further reflection, that he'd feel just as guilty about handing Jim over as he does about harboring him: "—s'pose you'd a done right and give Jim up; would you felt better than what you do now? No, says I, I'd feel bad—I'd feel just the same way I do now. Well, then, says I, what's the use you learning to do right, when it's troublesome to do right and ain't no trouble to do wrong, and the wages is just the same?"

Having written a letter denouncing Jim to Miss Watson, Huck tears it up and resolves to go to hell, where he can feel good about having harbored a runaway slave. Huck Finn, that situational ethicist, became my moral teacher, which he has remained. Trust your adulterated nature and do what comes handiest at the time. Huck's greatest disciple, Ernest Hemingway, sets forth the same code: "What is moral is what you feel good after and what is immoral is what you feel bad after." For my ethics, this has served.

Offered the chance to have life over again from the start, I know I'd say no. Young again? When the greatest satisfaction has been getting older? Young for what? To endure again the thousand natural shocks? When what I want now is to earn my grave? I've picked it out and the plot is paid for. Henry James tells, in his story "The Next Time," of a writer whom commercial success has eluded. The filigreed masterpieces of Ray Limbert are read by few. But then, through some blessing of old age, the siren voice of the market grows dim. He passes beyond ambition, lucky man; wakes up, amenable, "in the country of the blue," and stays there "with a good conscience and a great idea."

My own conscience is a mixed affair, like everyone's. But I believe it provides me with more occasions, marginally more, for feeling good about what I've done than for feeling bad. And like Limbert, I've got a great idea: to turn from trying to make this happen and that happen and have the future my way, and to bequeath myself instead to the sunlit, lavishly hospitable past, a country of the blue where I may bide what's left of my time.

Camp Indianola, 1964.

CHAPTER SEVEN

LAKE EFFECT

Deep into the Alzheimer's disease that would kill her in 2008 (as it had killed her father in 1970) my mother had moments of lucidity. The derelict circuits would briefly fire right and the articulate, reflective woman we had known would be suddenly among us again. In one of these interludes she told me that you really fall in love only once, which doubtless had been the case for her. These days I sleep badly and sometimes name in reverse order the forty-four Presidents of the United States, or else the twenty-six loves I've survived. Looking back across more than half a century, I see these as a chain of volcanoes, extinct by and large, though one or two still rumble. Mild commotions, very pleasant in the night.

Danny Metzinger had been first in the sequence. My great summer-camp love, Dickie Lippincott from Shaker Heights, Ohio, came directly after. By the shores of Lake Mendota, outside Madison, Wisconsin, with its network of lakes, was Camp Indianola, a Jewish boys' Shangri-la to which my parents sent me for four consecutive summers, starting when I was eight. Of the many things I thank them for, Indianola is near the top of the list. Unlike the other eight- and nine-year olds on either side of me in Cabin One that first summer, I could not be heard stifling sobs into my pillow after taps. Homesickness? My letters to Ranier Court were so disgracefully brief that my father finally wrote back in kind, saying: "We are fine too. Love, Daddy." Indianola was a first parcel of the great world I craved. The grass *was* greener in Wisconsin, the trees statelier, the air sweeter. I lived near enough to the ground and was enough of a naturalist to be very interested in the crawling life, whose variety outshone our Texas specimens.

Thus commenced my bill of particulars against home.

Captain Steve, my junior counselor in Cabin One, introduced us to Debussy, whose "Engulfed Cathedral" transported me. The record player in Cabin One resounded also with Tchaikovsky's *Pathétique* and Beethoven's Seventh. Returning home with such elegant new knowledge, I was a nine days' wonder to Mom and Dad, who enrolled me for piano lessons, an arduous season of which revealed no musical talent whatever.

Indianola's Native American motifs (not what anybody would have called them then) were widely standardized throughout the American summer-camp industry because of a single book, *Recreational Programs for Summer Camps* by H. W. Gibson. When I compare notes with former campers from other establishments, all testify to war paint, breechcloths, moccasins, tomahawks (one of which sits on my desk to this day), torchlight canoe races and the rest of it.

But putting a hand to one's mouth and saying "woo-woo-woo" was discouraged, to the credit of Chief Hank Woldenberg, owner of Indianola. At the climax of solemn campfires, after incantations and war dances, Chief, in a great headdress dragging the ground, would sweep into our gaze to deliver the benediction and send us, teary-eyed with camp love, to bed. "All is well," went our hymn, "safely rest, God is nigh." We wended our way with arms thrown over one another's shoulders, like drunks.

I remember "Calling Out," a majestic night ceremony at the climax of our color wars—Greens versus Whites—in which certain older boys were inducted into an esoteric society called the Order of Secret Merit. OSM for short. In the far meadow where Chief convoked us—with any luck, of a starry, moonless night—some Indian brave of the OSM would shoot a flaming arrow into the ground before each of the initiates. Thus were they "called out" and led away in awful silence to the deep woods. I knew as little about all this as I do today about Skull and Bones or Porcellian, but pictured, in the vague first blush of eros, a bacchanalia with war whoops and breechcloths flung up into the trees and unmentionable hoopla till break of day. In reality, about an hour after taps the inducted boys—shaken up, ennobled, possessed of the mysteries—were delivered back to their bunks. At reveille they rose as men.

It was in the summer of 1963, my third Indianola summer, when I was in Cabin Nine, that I met Dickie, who was in Ten. No boys like him in Fort Worth. Studying the planes of Dickie's face or watching his loose-limbed gait, I couldn't breathe right. He seemed to shed grace as he moved. I couldn't hear enough of his voice, which had a hairline crack in it. Radiantly at home with himself, Dickie was a stranger to coarseness or bullying. When we chose sides for any game, he as our natural leader would favor of all boys me, among Indianola's least coordinated.

I walked one morning before breakfast into Cabin Ten to find him in tears and hiding his face. Poor Dickie had wet the bed. Why were we younger campers so inclined to do this? A common morning sight was sheets hung out. Surely the unfamiliar atmosphere was to blame, the lake effect. Watching Dickie sob and fend me off with a flailing arm, I felt something break in me. I was in love and knew it.

All through the following school year I carried inside my shirt a snapshot of him in only his Speedo and Jack Purcells, and dreamed of our reunion in the coming summer of '64. (This snapshot was in fact on my person when I shook the President's hand.) Mom and Dad seemed unaware, but Mrs. Westbrook had noticed one day when I took it out to moon over. "Better put that picture away some-place where it won't get spoiled," she said, doubtless understanding more than I did about why I carried it. But I understood enough. As I saw it, Dickie and I were something like Dickie Loeb and Babe Leo-pold. But as good as they were bad. *My* Dickie and I would do wonders, not horrors. I was mad with excitement to be with him again.

Several days into the camping season of the fol-lowing summer I got a rude awakening. Another camper felt about Dickie as I did. This was Freddie Weymarsh of Knoxville, who supplanted me in one day's time. The camp went on a field trip. Dickie and I were assigned to different buses. When I got off mine, there he and Freddie were, thenceforth inseparable.

I swore never to get over it. And went where the brokenhearted go. To books. At Indianola the must-reads were *To Kill a Mockingbird*, *Lord of the Flies* and *The Catcher in the Rye*, a trinity standardized throughout the land. A few of the older boys were dipping into *Franny and Zooey* and *Nine Stories*. I even took a crack at *Seymour: An Introduction* but soon lost heart, skipping ahead to the magical last words: "Just go to bed, now. Quickly. Quickly and slowly."

That summer I finally did have tears to shed into my pillow. With boundless self-pity I'd go to bed quickly but to sleep slowly, indulging a good cry after lights-out; and did my utmost to suffer as much as I could; and, as usual, had murder in my heart, envisioning for Freddie a shallow culvert. I was indeed of the same clay as Loeb and Leopold. While you slept, Weymarsh, had you any idea how inclined I was to put a rag in your mouth?

A new friend came to my aid, bright-hearted, inquisitive Scott Simon, for many years now a much-loved personality on National Public Radio. But I hung upon his commentaries before any of you. He'd share with me pages of a novel he was at work on about a national political convention— which, as it happened, was what we were hearing on the radio each evening from San Francisco's Cow Palace. I'd go over to his cabin and sit on his bed till my welcome wore out, and listen to what we believed to be a real contest between Governor William Scranton of Pennsylvania and Senator Barry Goldwater of Arizona.

In reality it was only the leading Republican moderate, Governor Nelson Rockefeller of New York, who'd stood a chance against the Goldwater right. But Rocky had been outflanked. "Extremism in the defense of liberty" had triumphed. Scott the novelist took careful note of every rhetorical twist and turn. "It is essential that this convention repudiate here and now," shouted Rockefeller, who on the Tuesday evening of the convention had taken the podium to cheers and murmurs and a catcall or two, "any doctrinaire,"—here the boos began—"militant minority, whether Communist, Ku Klux Klan or Bircher"—cheers and boos—"which would subvert this party to purposes alien to the very basic tenets which gave this party birth." A deepening restiveness in the Cow Palace. "Precisely one year ago today, on July 14, 1963, I warned that the Republican Party is in real danger of subversion by a radical, well-financed and highly disciplined minority. . . ." Boos galore. "The methods of these extremist elements I have experienced at first hand—" Here a chorus of "We want *Barry!* We want *Barry!*" drowned out the governor.

Meanwhile, in New York, our national life took a dark turn on Thursday of that week: A fifteen-year-old black boy was shot in Harlem by a white policeman, precipitating six nights of large-scale looting and arson that spread also to the Bedford-Stuyvesant neighborhood of Brooklyn. Similar inner-city riots were shortly to follow in Rochester, Philadelphia, Chicago, Jersey City, Paterson and Elizabeth, along with one in St. Augustine, Florida. (Televised coverage of these events marked an epoch. "The other

America" was now on view every evening in middle-class homes. A summer later, in 1965, Watts was on fire. In 1966 it would be the Hough neighborhood of Cleveland. In 1967, Newark, Detroit, Milwaukee. During Holy Week of 1968, in the aftermath of Dr. King's murder, there were riots in more than a hundred American cities, our greatest national disorder since the Civil War. These urban devastations, along with a rapidly expanding presence in Southeast Asia and the growing antiwar movement it spawned, were what people would shortly mean by "The Sixties," when the air rang with utopian battle cries and stank of ghettos burning.)

Three weeks later that summer, at a little past ten-thirty on the night of August 4, about an hour after taps, I woke to the murmurs of several counselors on the veranda. They were tuning into a radio broadcast. I slipped from my covers and, hoping no floorboard would creak, padded to the screen door. The mournful voice of Lyndon Johnson was explaining that in the Gulf of Tonkin (wherever that was) an American destroyer, the USS *Maddox*, had been attacked with torpedoes two days earlier and two other destroyers had been attacked that day. And that we had sunk the offending gunboats and were retaliating further. "The determination of all Americans to carry out our full commitment to the people and to the government of South Vietnam will be redoubled by this outrage. Yet our response, for the present, will be limited and fitting. We Americans know, although others appear to forget, the risk of spreading conflict."

Here the President's voice grew emphatic: "We still seek no wider war."

There were quiet exchanges among the senior counselors, young men with only college deferments standing between them and conscription. "It is a solemn responsibility," the President wound up, "to have to order even limited military action by forces whose overall strength is as vast and as awesome as that of the United States of America, but it is my considered conviction, shared throughout your government, that firmness in the right is indispensable today for peace; that firmness will always be measured. Its mission is peace."

"Is there going to be a war?" I asked through the screen.

"Get back to bed!" one of the counselors ordered. I returned to my cot and drifted off, thinking of the godlike creatures on the veranda jumping out of helicopters and leaping from foxholes.

Earlier that day the bodies of three missing Congress of Racial Equality fieldworkers—Michael Schwerner, Andrew Goodman and James E. Chaney—were discovered in an earthen dam near Philadelphia, Mississippi. A day after that, in retaliation for the Gulf of Tonkin, American bombers carried out strike sorties against North Vietnamese torpedo bases and oil-storage depots at Hon Gai, Vinh and other coastal targets. What we now know, of course, is that the second Gulf of Tonkin attack never happened, that the *Maddox* and another vessel, the USS *Turner Joy*, had seen radar shadows, not torpedoes, on their instruments, and that the Gulf of Tonkin Resolution, Johnson's nearly unanimous warrant from

Congress for all the years of war to come, was based on a fiction. The bombing campaigns, the hundreds of thousands of ground troops, the free-fire zones and matter-of-fact atrocities, the widening of the war throughout Southeast Asia, the 58,307 American dead and hundreds of thousands maimed in body and mind, the uncountable Vietnamese dead—all of these the college boys on the veranda would in due course protest from the safety of their privileged lives. But as it was the first American war we sent chiefly our poor to fight and die in, I doubt that any of them ever went to Vietnam.

My constant companion from age nine had been a Nikkorex F 35mm. I became the best photographer at Indianola and won the photography competition two years running. My forte was pictures without people in them: close-up studies of lichens on stones; a broken fence entwined with poison ivy; canoes upside down in their racks. I still have some of these, printed with sepia toner to make everything look venerable. Already in childhood the perils of nostalgia were gaining on me.

But my masterpiece *did* have a figure in it. Under strictest supervision, I was allowed to go out on the rifle range and photograph Neil Meltzer lying prone with a .22 rifle pointed straight at me. This shot won the 1963 photography contest and appeared on the cover of the camp yearbook.

How am I remembered by those who were there? As a photographer, yes. Also as a purveyor of beside-the-point information, a tiptoe walker, a disaster at team sports and a furtive student of bodies in the communal showers. That I was asked back for three successive years after my rocky first summer is a tribute to the broad-mindedness of the management. I'd sometimes do bad things with no premeditation or even grasp of what I was doing. In my fourth and final summer I peed one morning out front of Cabin Sixteen rather than going to the lavatory, a terrible infraction. My cabin mates—none of whom cared for me, not even Dickie anymore—decided to administer the silent treatment. The silent treatment, from Dickie! Here was true desolation. Next evening Chief came to Cabin Sixteen's table in the refectory and told them to knock it off. His kindly words are with me still: "If all of us did what this boy did, the camp would smell like an open sewer. But it's time to forgive him. And to remember our own mistakes." Nobody had ever heard of Asperger's back then, of course. There were just us odd wads, spazzes, dipshits, homos, dickheads and so on. But Chief Woldenberg knew enough about boys to spot the peculiar one in need of a little looking after, a little latitude.

Still, he bore with me only up to a point. When my all-in-focus shot looking up a totem pole won me Indianola's photography competition for the second year in a row, he would not let it appear on the yearbook cover. "We've given him a prize for looking down the barrel of a gun," Chief said to Captain Dave, in charge of photography. "Now it's for looking up a totem pole. Frankly, I don't see any of that boy's photographs as prizeworthy."

How do I know Chief's words? I was eavesdropping under the window of his office. Truth was, the totem pole was magnificent, a great image I'm proud of to this day. But I was the embarrassing boy who'd peed on the green instead of in the can, and no more photos of mine were going to grace the yearbook cover.

CHAPTER EIGHT

NO JEWS, NO COMMIES, NO FAGS NEITHER

At the start of seventh grade in the autumn of 1964, perhaps in keeping with our changed circumstances, I passed from public into private school. Farewell, gentle high-minded Westcliff Elementary. Hello, brutal, snobbish Fort Worth Country Day.

Sensing the difficulties they'd plunged me into, my parents came up with their usual solution. A party. Mom and I addressed invitations to the whole seventh grade, none of whom I knew well: *"Come to a Patio Shindig!"* (*Shindig!* was a pop music show on TV that everybody was watching.) This was to be a boy-girl event, unimaginable only six months earlier. A shadow line had been crossed.

I prepared for the big evening by writing out and memorizing several things to say to my guests, whether they were interested to hear them or not. And a very satisfactory shindig it turned out to be, with the girls in their sweater sets and Dad turning hot dogs and hamburgers on the barbecue and a local disc jockey playing the top forty while my classmates and I wiggled. And everybody seeming to like me.

That was the week the Rolling Stones appeared for the first time on *Ed Sullivan*, singing "Time Is on My Side." A lot of other songs we danced to that evening have stood the test of time: "Twist and Shout" and "She Loves You," of course, by the greatest group of them all. And the Beach Boys' "I Get Around." But also the Supremes doing "Baby Love" and, for slow dancing, Chad and Jeremy's "A Summer Song," Dionne Warwick's "Walk On By," the Righteous Brothers' "You've Lost that Lovin' Feelin'" and—my favorite—Gerry and the Pacemakers' "Don't Let the Sun Catch You Crying."

True, we heard over and over on the radio the horrible novelty "My Boy Lollipop," a folk abomination called "We'll Sing in the Sunshine" and a demented bike-wreck ballad, "Leader of the Pack." But never to be forgotten from those music-rich months was "Then He Kissed Me" by the Crystals and Martha and the Vandellas' "Dancing in the Street." We were in a supernova of new music. The Negroes had taken charge of our emotions. Hearing the Drifters sing "Under the Boardwalk" or the Four Tops do "Baby I Need Your Loving" made the fifties-style white tunes of our elder siblings sound plain dumb.

Most of these songs advised a girl to put out. The penny may have dropped for two or three "couples" who ventured down the hill to exchange kisses and had to be called back by Mom, good-natured, unprudish, inclined to make a joke of such things, especially as we were, she believed, too young to know what came after a peck.

"It's *ice cream* up here!" she called into the autumn twilight. "All hands on deck!"

A few days after the party a boy named Fenton Bosley, who'd enjoyed himself on our patio, saw me sitting alone in the lunchroom—for the party hadn't made me as popular as it was intended to—and put down his tray next to mine. "Something I've been wanting to ask," he said. "Are you grateful?"

"Grateful for what?"

"For what we did for you."

"Did for me?" I asked. (Coming to my party?)

A quick pantomime as his face leapt into a snarl. "'Did for me?' The Second World *War*, queerbait. Don't you know we *fought* it for you people? Because you don't know how to fight."

Thus was I introduced to Jew-hatred. At dinner I told the folks what Fenton Bosley had said. Mom replied: "Bosley. The name registered with me when we were addressing invitations, but I didn't tell you. He's someone you knew when you were three and four. In nursery school. At the *synagogue*. But you knew him as Sammy." I remembered no Sammy or much else from when I was three and four. "After his father, Abe Epstein, went to New York and threw himself out the window of the Barbizon-Plaza, his widow, Lurleene, married Cliff Bosley and they changed the children's names, last and first. Sammy was the little boy and Ruthie was the little girl. He became Fenton, if you can believe it. She became Christine or something."

Poor Fenton, you perished a few years later in one of those flaming teenage car wrecks so common among the privileged of our town. A year or two more and Lurleene had shot Cliff to death after an evening at the country club where people witnessed him slap her around. (At that country club, Dad used to say, even the drapes were anti-Semitic.) No charges filed. I wonder what happened to the little girl. Probably nothing good.

Like every other classmate at Country Day, Fenton had been vociferous for Goldwater. Indeed, North Texas was at the center of the far-right strategy for defeating Rockefeller for the nomination. The whole ruling class of Fort Worth had gone over from the till recently omnipotent Democrats to this new breed of far-right Republicanism. They quoted from *The Conscience of a Conservative*, their savior's testament. (At the time nobody knew it had been ghostwritten for Goldwater by L. Brent Bozell Jr., William F. Buckley Jr.'s brother-in-law.) Many attended so-called resignation rallies at which they swore off sin, i.e., the Democratic Party, and were baptized into the gospel according to Barry. A decade after *Brown v. Board of Education*, the Supreme Court decision was deemed the devil's work: "I am firmly convinced," said Goldwater, "not only that integrated schools are not required, but that the Constitution does not permit any interference whatsoever by the federal government in the field of education." His Fort Worth followers damned civil rights as a "Second Reconstruction." Over drinks my classmates' parents discussed another of their favorite new books, John A. Stormer's *None Dare Call It Treason*, in which the federal government was unmasked as a bunch of Reds. And they more than muttered that the South was going to have to rearm.

As for the Civil Rights Act, signed into law by President Johnson in July, it prompted the inevitable outcry "States' rights, not civil rights!" along with boilerplate claims that the movement for racial equality was being run from Moscow. Lyndon Johnson's Great Society, his newly announced legislative program for the fight against poverty and racial discrimination, was seen as the Democrats' blueprint for a mongrelized Commie anthill. At Dallas Memorial Auditorium on June 16, when the Texas Republican State Convention gave Goldwater the fifty-six additional delegates he needed to clinch the nomination, he announced himself to the crowd as the only candidate for President "who is proud and happy to recognize the South as part of the United States." The wild demonstration that followed featured a banner, snake-danced through the hall, that read, "The worm has turned." It had indeed. The five states of the Deep South that

Goldwater would carry in November became the core of a Southern Strategy that gave Republicans their long-term edge in national politics. Foreseeing with great clarity the consequences of this southern shift, this turn of the worm, Johnson said privately: "If you can convince the lowest white man he's better than the best colored man, he won't notice you're picking his pocket. Hell, give him somebody to look down on, and he'll empty his pockets for you."

About a month before the election a strange news story gripped me and the nation. Johnson's closest aide, Walter Jenkins, was arrested for some kind of misbehavior in a men's room at the Washington, D.C., YMCA. "Must have had a nervous breakdown," I heard Dad tell Mom. "What the hell else could it be?" Goldwater supporters printed up bumper stickers saying ALL THE WAY WITH LBJ—BUT DON'T GO NEAR THE YMCA! I understood there was something ineffably nasty in all of this. And after that I would shudder when Dad warned Mom, as from time to time he did, that he was headed for a nervous breakdown. I believed he'd have to go to the Y to have it. And gathered that things went badly there.

On the morning of Election Day 1964, I covered my school blazer with Johnson–Humphrey buttons. When I came to breakfast Dad stared. "You're brave, son," was all he allowed. In chapel at Country Day the laughter around me was general. At lunch I ate alone, wondering if I should take off a few of the buttons. Breezing past on his way to the in-crowd's table, Fenton said: "For your information, Goldwater's got this thing wrapped up." That afternoon somebody, some fellow seventh-grader, I assume, stuck a note through the slot of my locker: NO JEWS, NO COMMIES, NO FAGS NEITHER.

I tore it into tiny pieces. I was ashamed. Not of the person who wrote it, of course. Of myself for having received it. I missed Westcliff and Mrs. Westbrook bad.

Next morning, November 4, the scene in chapel was hangdog. How on earth had Johnson won all but six states? Even Texas went for him. "For your information," Fenton told me (he was big on beginning sentences that way), "Johnson stole this whole thing." He had a very injured look on his face, which I wanted to wipe off. Had I been sixty-four and not twelve on that November morning, I'd have been armed with the wit to say: "Fenton, or Sammy, or whatever your name is, *this* election he did not steal."

Seventh grade wore on. Doing my damnedest to fit in, I bought a copy of *101 Ways to Popularity*, a manual for every teenage difficulty from acne to what to say to a friend whose father has gone to jail. I studied the gilded kids—how they walked and sat down and got up; how they cajoled and mocked and huddled; how they slightly modified the school uniform—in order to work out a style of my own. I needed loafers like Fritz's and a wristwatch like Pete's. But it was their *attitudes* I most longed to impersonate: their weary sarcasms, their humongous boredom, their pissed-off shrugs and merciless eye rolls. Oh, what was the point? I was neither sarcastic nor bored nor pissed off nor contemptuous. I was earnest, excited, eager to please. And explanatory.

Unbearably explanatory.

And a figure of fun, needless to say. I carried around—strictly for pretention—a copy of a book too rich for my blood or anybody's: *The Sound and the Fury.* "You read dumb things," said the prettiest girl in our grade, who went on to fame when she married the lead singer of the worst rock group of the seventies. (I assert this without fear of contradiction: The Eagles were the worst.) Still with me is that copy of Faulkner, defaced by a swastika some classmate drew on it. I attempted to make the insignia unrecognizable by turning it into four boxes.

Our physical education (and world history) teacher, Dennis Butz, a Dartmouth graduate and mouthy about it, had come under the spell of survivalism, recently popularized in the United States by favorable coverage of the Colorado Outward Bound School. In his mind we were not schoolboys but raw recruits. To please him we inched our way through corrugated tubes, rolled boulders uphill, climbed cargo nets and so on. Mr. Butz and Outward Bound were going to make men of us, and devil take the hindmost.

The hindmost was me. Butz packed his charges into the back of a pickup and drove into the wilderness due east of school. "Eat my dust!" he called out, raising a cloud of it as he abandoned us there. We ran hopefully west, I keeping up with the pack for a while. Then I found something too interesting not to examine, a horned frog and her babies in a nest. "Horny toads" had gotten scarce even then. The babies were perfect miniatures of their mother. I studied them awhile, then decided to catch up to the group. But there were brambles and stickers and now a fearsome itch began to migrate from my chin and neck and to fan out over my chest. The aura of an asthma attack. In no time I was fighting for air. I watched the rest of the boys vanish as a man overboard might watch his ship disappear.

My emergency pump—trade-named Medihaler in those days—was back in the locker room. Here I was, alone and suffocating and with no corticosteroid to inhale. The late-November air, crisp and sparkling, was all at once a mortal enemy. I tried to scream for help but as in a dream could not. Nor could I run. I was going to die. I was dying. I died.

And came to in the backseat of a strange car. In front were an elderly couple, Grant Wood's *American Gothic* by the look of them. The woman turned and said: "You need the hospital, sonny boy."

That there are angels afoot is not to be doubted. In the emergency room of All Saints, intravenous hydrocortisone saved me. Once I'd identified myself, my parents—my poor anguished parents, for it was by then eight or nine at night—were phoned. I do remember having been in the farmer's arms when we arrived. And in my father's arms next morning when I was discharged. My parents had spent the night with me. The farmer and his wife had slipped away without identifying themselves and we didn't learn their names or how they came upon me after I lost consciousness. I am ashamed to say that decades go by without my thinking of them.

A weekday evening, not long after my close shave. Mom's watchful eye is on me. We've finished dinner in the kitchen. I am starting to clear. The doorbell rings. Aunt Vera, my mother's older sister, and her gargantuan and deranged husband, Isadore Wolchansky—Uncle Walnuts—come in silently. I make myself scarce, as always when that lunatic is in the house. Once, with nobody else in earshot, he said to me: "You're too pretty." I knew this was not seduction but insult.

Isadore's self-pity can readily turn to rage, as it is about to this evening. All at once he's beating on my father. My mother and Vera are screaming. As always when scared, I am under my desk, hands over my ears, though I hear Walnuts shout from the living room, "Come back and fight!" as Dad barrels down the hall and slams his bedroom door. I peek out from Peru and see a red hand smear on the wall. Isadore has bloodied Dad. The only bloodshed ever known under our roof. I hear my mother, in an unfamiliar voice, ordering Isadore and Vera *out*. For one terrible moment, I wonder if he's going to hit her too. Then I hear the Wolchanskys slam the front door, slam their car doors, roar off.

You'd think after screams and fouled walls and slamming doors there would be some attempt to explain to the boy in the corner bedroom what has happened. Do Mom and Dad think I haven't heard? Am I meant not to notice his ravaged nose and her red eyes?

Tommy gets home quite late. The rest of us are already asleep. Next morning at breakfast he looks at Dad and says: "What the hell happened to you?"

"Well, son, I was reaching for some files on a high shelf and—"

"You look like you've been in a fight."

Dad went on telling people his feeble story about files on a high shelf till his nose healed.

This Uncle Walnuts drama can have been only about money. He had a gift for making it vanish. He and Aunt Vera and their three sons had come from Shreveport and moved in with my grandparents, ostensibly to care for my failing grandmother but in reality because they were destitute. The last thing my dying Bubbe needed was a houseful of Wolchanskys. I believe this was the reason she came to live with us briefly in the fall of 1960: a little respite from her obsessive, unpredictable son-in-law and his misbegotten attempts at help-fulness, which never failed to make things worse.

On the path of a new mania, Isadore set up a pair of aquariums in her and Grandpa's bedroom. These were meant to spread enchantment. Listen-ing to them gurgle in the night, Little Bubbe turned her face to the wall. In one of the spare rooms upstairs was a pair of bedsteads carved with swans above the scrollwork—the beds my mother and her younger sister, Sylvia, had slept in as girls. Walnuts sawed the swans off. When she saw what he'd done, Mom couldn't hold back her tears. Other desecrations, billed by Walnuts as improve-ments, were to follow. With such people you have no idea what's coming next.

Little Bubbe died in May of 1961, ravaged and spectral and a few months older than I am now. It was my first death. I watched Mom grieve wildly, for she and Bubbe had been something like the

Little Bubbe and Grandpa with their children
and grandchildren, early 1961.

mother and grandmother in Proust, seeing each other every day, finding it difficult to part. We'd drop by Bubbe's after school. After half an hour Mom would look at her watch and say we had to go. Bubbe would walk us out to the car, then remember something she needed to show Mom. We'd go back in. New topics would be broached. The telephone would ring and, after Bubbe's lengthy conversation with cousin Becky, whose latest medical problem had to be thoroughly reported to Mom, along with cousin Becky's update on the declining health of cousin Molly, Bubbe would accompany us back to Mom's car, where fresh matters were introduced. I am told that this routine is familiar in Bengali clans and I have observed it for myself in Southern Italy. Brazilians, too, are slow to part. Good-bye without leaving is a worldwide tradition, to which my mother and grandmother strongly adhered.

When Little Bubbe died she took the family compass with her. Nothing was ever good again at 2225 Windsor Place. Grandpa declined quickly into dementia, first confused about recent events, later convinced he was back in Sielce, the Polish town northwest of Lublin that he'd left with his parents in 1904. When he could no longer manage the stairs a hospital bed was installed in the living room with round-the-clock nurses. Aunt Vera and Uncle Isadore now lived in what had been his and Bubbe's bedroom. On the night of August 10, 1967, almost three years after the bloody altercation at our house, the phone rang and Nurse Baylis, Grandpa's night attendant, told my mother she'd heard a single shot overhead. Mom made the fifteen-minute drive to Windsor Place to find that Uncle Isadore had blown his brains out in an upstairs bathroom.

My father refused to be a pallbearer though he offered Aunt Vera what help he could. I know I'd rejoice in the suicide of anyone who had hit me on the nose. But Dad declined to gloat and never again referred to Isadore as Uncle Walnuts.

CHAPTER NINE

A STATUTE OF LIMITATIONS

Most Saturdays I got the whole day for book-worming at our downtown library. Dad would drop me off and not return for hours. I only needed to be on the front steps by four. Whereas the atmosphere in Fort Worth's suburban branch libraries tended to be lax, downtown it was strict because of the head librarian, Miss Longstreth, a righteous terror who stalked around on spindle shanks to reprimand talkers and even note-passers and who always looked as if she'd smelled something bad. One afternoon, tucked away in the stacks, I lost track of the time and Dad had to come in to find me. (Surely better than having to roust your boy from a pool hall.) I recall that I was seated on the floor, doing nothing more blameworthy than reading without proper light, when suddenly Miss Longstreth and Dad were telling me to be more aware of the hour and stop being so self-centered and act more like a big boy and so on.

Five minutes later, turning to me out on the street with manly confidentiality (and unaware that his hairpin turns from anger to mirth were what I dreaded most), Dad said Miss Longstreth would "die wondering," which took some working out but I got it.

I hoped she wouldn't die before recommending a few more good books. "This one is usually suggested to the girls," she'd told me about *My Ántonia*, "which makes no sense since it's mostly about a boy." Here was something I really could read, unlike the Faulkner. In the weekday wasteland of Country Day I held fast to Cather's masterwork, and failed to hand it back on the due date, incurring a fifty-cent fine and getting the full Longstreth treatment. In the novel an orphaned and displaced Virginia boy, Jim

Burden, fetches up on the Nebraska plains. "There was nothing but land: not a country at all but the material out of which countries are made." What amazed me, I recall, was the story of Peter and Pavel, immigrant farmhands from the Ukraine. Theirs is but one of the cultures and languages on the sparsely inhabited prairie—a babel like that in and around Cather's childhood home of Red Cloud. Russians, Czechs, Poles, Swedes, Jews, Lapps, Mexicans, and other immigrant nationalities dotted the Nebraska landscape. They had been Cather's first claim on cosmopolitanism, and she held this early exposure dearer than any she would gain later on.

Bad luck dogs Pavel and Peter: debts, illness. Misfortune has settled like an evil bird on the roof of their log house, flapping its wings there, warning people away. As Pavel lies dying, he imparts their atrocious secret to Jim Burden and Jim's great friend, Ántonia Shimerda:

After wedding festivities in a neighboring Ukrainian village, Pavel and Peter led a bridal party home in an escort of sledges. A rout of wolves— famished, hundreds strong—descended upon them from a dark line of trees and drove one of the sledges aground. Screams of agony filled the night as the hungry beasts leapt to their prey. Then more wolves caused a second sledge to go over. More bloodcurdling cries. More wolves. A third sledge was attacked. The groom watched as his father, mother and sisters were set upon. Now only the first sledge, carrying the bride and groom—and Pavel and Peter—remained. Wolves were abreast of them. The horses shrieked in terror. Peter bluntly told the groom they must lighten, and pointed to the bride. "The young man cursed him and held her tighter. Pavel tried to drag her away. In the struggle, the groom rose. Pavel knocked him over the side of the sledge and threw the girl after him. . . . Peter, crouching in the front seat, saw nothing. The first thing either of them noticed was a new sound that broke into the clear air, louder than they had ever heard it before—the bell of the monastery of their own village, ringing for early prayers."

Such is the shame that has harried Pavel and Peter to Nebraska.

For Jim and Ántonia the farmhands' story—a

glimpse into the worst life can do—has no end to it, for such glimpses grant, along with horror, a different emotion, "as if the wolves of the Ukraine had gathered that night long ago, and the wedding party been sacrificed, to give us a painful and peculiar pleasure." In the end, every inspection of the worst becomes a durable story told by firelight to the warm and well-fed. Thus literature is born and reborn. No end to its pleasures. But what they start with is somebody's hell.

These were not things I or any twelve-year-old could know. I received the book at my twelve-year-old level. But some seed of Cather's must have fallen on fertile ground. *My Ántonia* has stayed with me in all its particulars, from Jim Burden's arrival at the white frame house of his grandparents to his return, decades later, as a New Yorker and man of the world. The action of the novel is an unforgetting, with Jim's remote prairie past, stored away for years while he forged a brilliant career, rising up to reclaim him: "Whenever my consciousness was quickened, all those early friends were quickened within it, and in some strange way they accompanied me through all my new experiences."

The future is dark, the present a knife's edge. It's the past that is knowable, incandescent, real. Here is an instance, looming up from darkness the way involuntary memories do, untouched for years yet as fresh as when it happened:

One night that autumn of 1964, as I labored in vain over something called the New Math that Country Day was inflicting, our phone rang and I happened to pick up at the same moment as Dad in his office. A lady's voice said, very casually, "You want to meet me?" Dad said he did indeed. A few minutes later he was putting on his hat and coat and telling Mom he had to see a businessman from out of town about a deal.

After several hours of terrible confusion in Peru, I decided he'd gone to see a businessman from out of town with a lady's voice. I put this away, along with so much of the past, for half a century, and am taking it out only now. It cannot hurt anyone anymore, including me. Now it's just a painful and peculiar pleasure. Dad admired women wildly—but gallantly, I believe. Oh, I am certain, and only when

Mom wasn't around. When she was, he kept custody of his eyes. In her presence the most he would say about another woman was, "She's pretty well put-together." Extramarital activity was the dark side of his moon. At the funeral were a couple of weeping women none of us recognized.

Something from August 1964. Let it stand here, a little out of sequence, as My Best Moment, My Ninety-five Theses, My Declaration of Independence, My Coming into My Own (loveliest phrase in the language), My Epitome:

I am just home from Indianola and we are promptly on our way to the Mayo Clinic in Rochester, Minnesota—which seems to me a poor excuse for a holiday, but Mom is in chronic pain and the Fort Worth doctors can't seem to get to the bottom of it. We already have a good deal of history with the Clinic, admiration for which is among Dad's cardinal tenets. "The Supreme Court of Medicine," he never tires of saying. There Bubbe Bockstein's nephritis had been diagnosed in the late fifties and her poor prognosis given. There Grandpa Bockstein was treated at the onset of his dementia. "Let's all get checkups while we're there. You too, son."

"But there's nothing wrong with me."

"You too."

We're traveling by car. "On a long car trip there's time to talk everything over. Nothing better for a family than a thousand miles in the car," says Dad. Another unshakable tenet. By the end of the arduous first day we've made it from Fort Worth to Excelsior Springs, Missouri. We check into The Elms, a broken-down spa where generations of Missourians once came to take the medicinal waters. The place has historic significance. On the evening of November 2, 1948, election night, President Harry Truman traveled with four Secret Servicemen from Independence to The Elms, checked in, borrowed a robe and slippers from the proprietor, got a steam bath and a rubdown, ate a ham-and-cheese sandwich, drank a glass of buttermilk and put himself to bed. The world assumed Governor Thomas E. Dewey of New York was about to unseat him, but Truman was awakened a little before dawn and told he'd carried twenty-eight states to Dewey's sixteen. The President and his detail checked out early and drove home to Independence.

We check out early too. Rochester is six hours away. We grab breakfast at one Stuckey's in Iowa, lunch at another, and arrive before nightfall. Early the next day Mom begins her round of examinations. Quickly enough, the doctors determine that she has a bleeding ulcer, exacerbated by months of the large doses of aspirin she's been taking. It doesn't speak well of her Fort Worth doctors that such a simple diagnosis has proved beyond their competence.

The doctors I am to see include an allergist, an otolaryngologist, a pulmonologist, an oncologist (the reason for whom has of course been kept from me), a psychiatrist, an orthopedist and a podiatric surgeon.

It is only in the course of this final appointment that my composure breaks.

"Heel, toe! Heel, toe!" has been the household refrain ever since I began walking. My parents, who love me (maybe even best), have never reconciled themselves to my tiptoeing ways, which are the family consternation. Here I am at twelve, still hearing "Heel, toe!" When I was five and six they'd put me in orthopedic clodhoppers with metal plates in the soles and steel braces running up the legs. To this day when I see a photo of Franklin Roosevelt that shows braces peeking from under the cuffs of his trousers, I feel sorry for myself instead of him.

Dad and I make ourselves comfortable in the podiatric surgeon's office. Dad starts in with his usual palaver about how well I do in school. Meanwhile the doctor, who's all business, is drawing a picture of my feet on his chalkboard.

"This boy has *quite* a vocabulary," Dad tells him, "and is a lover of grand opera and can name the kings of England going way back."

The surgeon nods and explains, without trimmings, how a simple slicing of the Achilles tendons will allow me to walk like other boys.

Or never walk again? As I rise from my chair I think I hear, through a mental roaring, Dad go on about "this boy's ability to identify the constellations." There I stand with mouth agape, but no big vocabulary coming out. Is my father so busy with parental pride that he's not heard the stupefying thing this white-coated divinity just said? "And we've got a historical atlas you can't keep him out of. His mother says—"

I pick up my chair and hurl it at the surgeon.

A blur of noise and motion follows. What I know next is that my father is on top of me. In despair. But in tenderness, I feel. In pity.

In fear. It is the moment he knows I am not his invention but something unaccountable. What I am trying to say with that chair, I think he understands:

That I am *correct* as nature made me.

Pinned beneath his two hundred twenty pounds, I know I've won—I have the proof that I can frighten him. When we do get up it is to make a hasty exit. From Dad the doctor gets a profuse apology and assurances that we'll be in touch. From me he gets a homicidal stare. Obeying my adulterated nature, trusting to what comes handiest, I have defeated family and clinic at one go. No "heel, toe, heel, toe" about it as we left. I must have pranced, feeling good as Huck when he decided to go to hell.

My mother died less than eight weeks after my father in 2008. I wanted certain of her belongings to go to my women friends. Frances Kiernan occasionally carries a little evening bag with garnets on the clasp. Patricia Volk can be seen in an Hermès scarf she wears as an ascot. Molly Haskell looks terrific in a black knit party dress trimmed in gold thread. Amy Hempel sports an ivory-colored Bottega Veneta shoulder bag. Alison West has the gown of shot beads over chiffon that Mom wore on her and Dad's forty-fifth wedding anniversary.

To see these relics out and about is a great solace. I'd hoped also to pass along Mom's many pairs of shoes, a lot of them unacquainted with the pavement, but could find nobody who wore size 6 triple A. The dress size too—which was 2—made most of her dozens of dresses, an abecedarium of postwar fashion, hard to give worthily away. Only one woman I knew was small enough to fit into most of them: Junie Fischbein. A notable clotheshorse in her own right, Junie is notable for other things, too, chief among them broken friendships.

Violent disdain after early fascination is her trade-mark. Borderline personality, the doctors call this. We were briefly cordial before I joined (for reasons never clear to me and about which I'm not curious) the ranks of her ex-friends.

Yet I believe that several of Mom's dresses hang to this day in Junie's closet. Our paths cross only four or five times a year, but she makes the most of these occasions, snubbing me brutally if I try to say hello or casting a theatrical glance my way as she whispers some calumny into the ear of a not yet ex-friend. Peace to her. She's seen a lot of trouble: visits to the loony bin, collapsed facelifts and more. But if I were to come upon Junie Fischbein in my sainted mother's clothes, I'd tell her off and feel newborn.

Nothing experienced is ever gone, only submerged. The least detail waits upon unprompted recollection. New pieces of the shipwreck surface even as I relinquish this book. Here is a photo of Mom at some sort of Fort Worth cotillion. The year is 1936. She's a senior in high school like the other girls in the picture, all of whom I will know later as middle-aged ladies of the community. That movie star–like creature to Mom's right is Shirley Ginsburg, who'll be Robby Anton's mother. On the far left is Charlotte Miller, looking angelic under a veil. (She was anything but angelic.) My mother has the best smile of them all. The following year she'll go to Louisiana State University at Baton Rouge, where Robert Penn Warren will be one of her teachers; he must have been writing *All the King's Men* at the time. Then on to the University of Texas at Austin.

But it was marriage and motherhood she was after, not higher learning. Back in Fort Worth in the summer of 1940, she got a call from a boy from Tyler up on a visit—very dashing and impetuous, a storyteller, a showboat and braggart, a diamond in the rough—and fifteen minutes into their first date, before they even got where they were going, he clapped his hands together at the steering wheel and said, "I got an idea! Let's you and me get married!" She went home and phoned Shirley: "That boy is completely out of his mind." But six months later she was on her

Annette Bockstein and friends, November 1936.

father's arm, walking down the aisle in the Hotel Texas ballroom. With a hundred-and-two-degree fever, very evident in surviving photos. Look at her, she's a wreck. Dad, on the other hand, looks like the guy who's caught the brass ring.

Which he has.

Once Mom was over her flu they drove to New Orleans for a belated honeymoon. The bridal suite of the Roosevelt was what she had in mind. Dad booked them into a little motor court instead. "You're father's not paying for this honeymoon, I am," he explained. But there were dinners at Antoine's and Galatoire's, strolls along Bourbon Street and in Jackson Park. I don't think they knew each other very well yet.

Back to Fort Worth they came, but with no bun in the oven. The clock ticked. No bun. Spring, summer, fall. Nothing. Then the Japanese attacked Pearl Harbor and within four weeks Mom was pregnant. This must have occurred the world over—young marrieds determined to make hay while the sun shone.

Dad joined the Navy. Tight-lipped afterward about his wartime experience, like so many of

Petty Officer Taylor.

those men, he left me only a few bones from which to reconstruct the dinosaur:

He could not swim, this able-bodied seaman, and had a terrible fear of all bodies of water, even swimming pools. My own love of swimming (the only athletic skill I had other than the fifty- and the hundred-yard dash) was a source of pride to him. Among the few Navy stories he did tell was how one day, on calm seas, a patch of water was set alight with kerosene and the enlisted men forced to swim under the flames. It was the only time Dad swam in his life and may have contributed to the hydrophobia that Mom—another natural swimmer—and I laughed about freely when the old man was out of earshot.

I lose track of him for a couple of years, then pick him up again in the Philippines campaign of 1944–1945, by which time he held the rating of Petty Officer First Class, with storekeeping duties, on a destroyer escort. I have in an old trunk his dress-blue service uniform, scratchy as a horse blanket. Dad's convoy was anchored off Mindanao and saw action in the battle of Leyte Gulf, Japan's last naval stand. He was somewhere in the South China Sea on April 13, 1945, when his CO came onto the public address to announce FDR's death. The new commander in chief was a failed haberdasher from Missouri. Strong men wept with fear.

A month after the end of the war he celebrated Rosh Hashanah in Manila. In one of those astounding wartime coincidences, my uncle Fred Schwartz, an Army man, Aunt Sylvia's husband, heard Dad's unmistakable East Texas burr amid the observant throng. Though they couldn't abide each other, soldier and sailor fell into—what else?—a tearful hug.

By any measure, Mom and Dad and Tommy had an excellent war. When Petty Officer First Class Taylor got a stateside leave to Los Angeles, the three kept house in what was then called the Beverly Wilshire Apartment Hotel—two kids with a kid and a whole Pacific of luck on their side.

What is this joy I get from thinking of them without me? All are dead now and a statute of limitations applies. No more misunderstanding, recrimination, rage, blame—or grief. I am a sixty-four-year-old

The three of them, winter 1942–43.

smiling man on a bench at the Central Park Zoo, making of the bones what I can. If you need to find me, here's where to look, whatever the season. It's a fifteen-minute walk from the apartment where I live. Should I happen to die here, that'll be all right.

Parents and children gather round the Delacorte Clock. When monkeys ring the hour, a horn-playing kangaroo, snare-drummer penguin, tambourine-shaking bear, violinist hippo, concertina-playing elephant and panpiper goat go round and round and make the children squeal with pleasure.

All I want is to be gathered into this sudden bliss of solitude. Chance, imponderable chance! I could as easily be another sort of park-bench man. The one I am is grateful to the full: to be still an undiseased mind in an undiseased body; to be at last without remorse (which will gnaw you good if you let it); to have loved and labored, and under no curse; to have watched the happiness of others.

In my mother's last lucid episode, about nine months before her death, she said some things I hurriedly wrote down: "This is a hard sickness to take. I just want a regular happy home, each in his own family and back to normal. What's the reason for this? Can't you get me out? I don't think I can hold up for much more." And after a pause: "Do you see any settlement in sight?"

What has happened cannot be made not to have happened. What has happened cannot happen again. My mother was born fifty days after my father in the summer of 1919 and died fifty-four days after him in the spring of 2008.

Their having been here defies all undoing.

December 26, 1940.

Naples Declared

A Walk Around the Bay

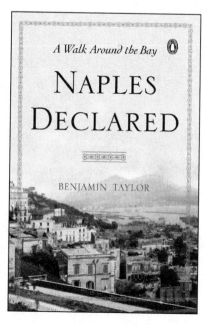

Gracefully written and full of good humor, *Naples Declared* presents a compulsively readable account of three thousand years of Naples history. From the catacombs of San Gennaro to the luminous paintings of Caravaggio to the ruins of Pompeii in nearby Campania, renowned author Benjamin Taylor takes readers on a stroll around the city Italians lovingly call Il Cratere.

"There is no more witty, worldly, cultivated, or amiably candid observer imaginable than Benjamin Taylor. This book belongs on the shelf of the very best literary travel guides." –Phillip Lopate

PENGUIN BOOKS   prh.com/nextread